From the first time I spoke with Allison, I felt like I knew her. I could tell she was a woman of deep faith, deep thought, and very deep intelligence. The only thing I didn't know was her story.

After reading *Faith and Forgiveness*, I knew exactly why I felt as if I knew Allison before I knew her story. God's Spirit was in control of her life and His Presence was unmistakable. Deep calls unto deep.

About two years later, she came to my office and shared that she had written a book. With trembling hand, she gave me the memory stick and asked if I would read it.

Well…I wasn't prepared for the deep impact it was going to have. I started and finished it in one sitting. No one will be able to read this book and stay the same. She beckons us to go higher with God to full freedom. The best part is that she takes us on her journey, step by step, and her story is living proof that it is possible.

So if the Son sets you free, you will be free indeed. John 8:36

Terri Broome
Director of Women's Ministry, Pursuit Church, Denver NC
Author of *The Ordinary Road*

Faith &
Forgiveness

Allison D. Pelphrey

Faith & Forgiveness

Copyright © 2019 by Allison D. Pelphrey

All rights reserved.

Printed in the United States of America

ISBN13: 978-1-79816-168-5

DEDICATION

For my children, Aaron and Autumn. You've always inspired me to
be a better version of myself, and to take the journey towards
healing and freedom. I love you more than words can ever express.
I pray that your lives will be full and happy, but more than anything
that you walk with God.

My daughter, Autumn – inspiration for book cover

ACKNOWLEDGMENTS

Special thanks:

To Terri Broome, a fearless woman of God, who inspires so many to live open, authentic lives. I so appreciate your guidance, prayers, and encouragement through this process!

To Maria Greene, for all the encouragement and prayers, and for taking the time to edit my work!

To Sharon Fox @Sharon Fox Photography, for doing such a great job on the author pic!

To Stacy Dodd @ Tater Design for the fabulous book cover!

Tater Design

937-522-5888

Instagram & Facebook handle: @Taterdesignss

Email: taterdodddesigns@gmail.com

To the many women who have impacted my life over the years, my heart-felt love and thanks for believing in me and encouraging me each step of the journey.

CONTENTS

1 FOREWORD

Prov 28:13 NLT – People who conceal their sins will not prosper, but if they confess and turn from them, they will receive mercy.

Until recently, I had never encountered Christians who readily talk about their sins. Like my past self, most of us are experts at burying our sins and putting on a facade. We pretend that our little Christian life is perfect, and while we make "mistakes", we dare not come clean about our failures (sins – let's call it what it is), for fear of judgement. Even though the scripture tells us in ***James 5:16 Confess our sins, one to another, and pray for each other***, we justify our silence by telling others "I'm just a private person" (guilty!). The fact is, we don't want people to know our ugly truths. I sure didn't look forward to exposing mine. When we expose our inner-most beings, we become vulnerable and we lose control. Here's some hard truth. You were never in control! If God is not in control of your life, then Satan most certainly is!

I was hesitant to write this for fear of judgement and even loss of relationships by many who will read what I've done, and focus more on my past sins, than on the work that God has done in my heart or the prospects of the future He has in store for me. But God challenges us in ***Joshua 24:15 Choose ye this day whom ye serve***. Do I serve God or man? As for me, I serve God and will not fear what man can do. If I lose relationships due to the truths within, I will miss them. But I have God, and with Him at the helm of my life, I fear nothing, and I gain everything.

2 FAITH HERITAGE

I've come to appreciate that the most important gift we can give to our children and future generations is that of a Christ-centered heritage. I'm blessed that I've experienced that in my family. Let me set the stage by giving you some background on my family. My father's mother, Murzie, was known to be a godly woman. She left behind a legacy of strong character and a love for God that impacted, all eight of her children. My grandfather, Frank, abandoned the family when my father was in the 8th grade. So, my dad, her eldest, had to quit school to go to work in the coal mines to support his mother and younger siblings. While I'm sure this was a tough time for my father, I also believe it instilled a strength of character and strong ethics that would follow him, his entire life. My father, Earl Pelphrey, was the greatest influence in my life. Except for Jesus Christ, I still believe he's the greatest man that ever lived. Simply put, as a child, he was my hero.

He and mama were childhood sweethearts. They met when daddy was age 15 and mama was age 14. The story is that he told her the day he met her that he was going to marry her, and he courted her from then, on. But at the age of 18, he was shipped overseas to fight in World War II. After fighting in the African campaign for several months, he was sent to Europe to fight as well. The story I always heard as a child was that his platoon found themselves surrounded by the Germans. My father, and his friend, chose to swim across the river to run phone cable, so that they could call for reinforcements. They got the cable ran and the call was made. But he and his friend were captured before they could swim back to their platoon. He suffered greatly at the hands of the Nazi's for the remainder of the war, as he spent the last months of the war in one of their prison camps. He came home from the war, angry and damaged by all the atrocities he had experienced and witnessed. The war had made him hard.

My parents were married shortly after dad returned home from the war, on June 27, 1945, and began raising our family. My older siblings knew a tough father, who was very strict and often severe at times. However, just after I was born (twenty years after the war), he gave his heart to Christ. While my older siblings grew up with a "grizzly" bear as a father, I only knew him to be a "teddy" bear.

Christ had healed him from all the hurts and had softened this very hard man and molded him into His servant. He was called to ministry soon after he was born again, in 1966. He became an Evangelist and the godliest person I've ever known. He had an immovable faith that marked my life from my earliest memories to this day. He was a pillar of the community in our home town, Paintsville, Kentucky. He was loved and respected by everyone that met him. Not only did people seek him out in life for godly counsel, or to preach and teach God's Word, but upon his death, hundreds of people came to his funeral; a real testament to the impact he had on so many lives.

My mother, Pauline, was a hard-working, stay at home mom, who had suffered great brokenness and rejection in her early years. She was born out of wedlock, in the 1920's. From her stories, I learned that she had been abused, and except for her great grandmother's attention, she was denied affection by the rest of her family for most of her childhood. Her mother (aka: Granny, who by the time I came along, looked and acted a lot like Granny Clampett from "The Beverly Hillbillies"!), had basically dropped her off with her own parents, who mistreated my mother.

My mother grew up knowing she was not wanted by the stoic Scottish, McKenzie family, because of her illegitimacy. Mama told me that it was her, great grandmother, Mindy, (who she thought was a Cherokee woman) who nurtured and kept her alive the first ten years of her life. Grandma Mindy was 80 years old when my mom came to live with them as an infant. She died at the age of 90, when mama was only ten years old. Mama was convinced, had it not been for her Grandma Mindy, she would not have lived.

After Mindy's death, mama's life became even more challenging and she basically had to fend for herself, still living with her grandparents. She would arrive home from school, after dark, and find the dinner table full of dirty dishes, which she was expected to clean, and no food left for her to eat. She survived by eating the scraps off the dirty plates. She finally went to live with her mother when she was a teenager.

She gave birth to nine children of her own. So, by the time I (number nine) came along, mama was exhausted. Regardless of her internal struggles, I know she loved God and I know Jesus lived in her heart. After all she was the one who taught me the power of prayer. But in her brokenness, sometimes she would have what I call "melt downs". Never did she hurt any of us kids physically, but instead she would threaten to hurt herself – even to end her own life. Several times I witnessed daddy calmly talking her "down off the ledge".

The memories of seeing my mom in so much distress dug at the core of me. Even though she had her own demons to battle, she was a godly woman who believed in the power of prayer and taught me to pray about everything.

3 MY SPIRITUAL JOURNEY BEGINS

Proverbs 22:6 Start children off on the way they should go, and even when they are old, they will not turn from it.

My life began in 1965, when I was born, the youngest of nine kids. However, my spiritual story began when I was three years old – actually, a couple of months before my fourth birthday.   Our family was living in Dayton, Ohio at the time. It was Christmas, 1968 and I vividly remember galloping around our home, on my new stick pony I had gotten for Christmas that morning.   Over my childhood, mama would tell me the story about how I suddenly stopped, looked out the window and said, "There's no snow! Mama, where's the snow!?!".   I guess I fully expected that with Christmas, there would be snow. However, it was unseasonably warm for Ohio that winter and there was no snow in sight.   My mother suggested I pray and ask God to let it snow.   In my very childlike way, I did just that; I prayed and asked God to let it snow. And then I carried on riding my new stick pony.

A few hours later, as we sat down to dinner, my sister, Yvonne, said, "Neicie, look!", as she pointed to the window in disbelief.   There it was, the snow I had prayed for was gently falling! I still remember the awe and excitement I felt knowing that God heard me! In that moment, this God, whom I had only heard stories about, became real to me!   I asked for snow and HE, the Almighty I heard my parents talk about so often, sent it - for

ME! I know that in that moment, the Holy Spirit planted a seed of faith in me and He marked my life. From then on, I had a knowledge of God's presence which has never left me over my life - even during moments of doubt when I felt very much alone – even in those moments when I tried, so hard, to push Him away. That seed of faith continues to grow to this day.

A difficult lesson I've observed over the years, is that every time God moves in our life or when he puts an anointing on a person, as I believe He did me, the enemy, Satan, is there to try to snatch the good away. Just a few short months after my very special encounter with God, I experienced evil for the first time. The summer after my fourth birthday, I was sexually abused by a couple of the neighborhood boys. Even in my innocence, I knew that what was happening to me was so wrong. That event was seared into my memory and an indelible scar was etched into my soul. I never spoke a word to anyone about what happened. That was the beginning of my learning to keep secrets.

As I think back, it's mind-boggling that a four-year old could experience such a deep level of shame, but I did. I remember my mom instructing me to keep my privates "private" and now, her number one rule had been violated, not by me, but by others. I internalized the blame and the shame, even though it was completely out of my control (control freak roots planted here!). From this terrible event, fear was one of the earliest strongholds that took root. I began having vivid night terrors that stuck with me into my teen years. Thankfully, the abuse by those boys, happened only once. A year or so later, my parents moved our family back to the family farm in Kentucky. I loved Kentucky. I loved the mountains and how they seemed to wrap their arms around me and offer a sense of peace and protection. There in the hills of Eastern Kentucky, life was good…for a while.

I started school at Flag Gap Elementary when I was five, where I met my lifelong friend, Martha Hampton. We also attended the same church, Little Mud Lick Church of God. I was thrilled to get to see her most days of the week. This period of my life was good, but again, I experienced more pain and confusing times – this time at home. I was torn about whether to include this, not wanting to disrespect my mother's memory in any way, but in the spirit of transparency, and knowing where she is today, I feel I must. Especially since these events affected me and even led to some generational curses.

As I mentioned before, my mother had suffered a lot of brokenness in her youth. In one of the worst episodes I witnessed, my mother, feeling exhausted and unappreciated by everyone, had one of her melt-downs. At first, she threatened to hurt herself. I remember seeing her hold this large, curved knife. I wasn't sure what she intended to do with it, but the sight of it in her hands while she was so upset, terrified me. Eventually, daddy calmed her down. So then, she just decided she was going to leave. My brother and I (the two youngest) were hanging onto our Granny in the living room, crying and afraid of what was happening in the next room. After a while, mama called us into the kitchen, where they were talking, and told us she was leaving, and we had to choose between her and daddy. My brother immediately stepped to her side, while I clung and even hid behind daddy. I think it shocked her that I didn't run to her. Shortly after that, the episode ended, and she didn't leave, but she became withdrawn from me.

I loved her, and I believe she knew that, but after that moment – after that choice - things were never quite the same between us. She didn't speak to me for about two weeks. I didn't understand then that she was looking for affirmation and my actions were seen by her as rejection. In my heart I wasn't rejecting her, but honestly, all I remember is the fear I felt and the sense of peace I always had with my dad. Finally, I apologized to her and told her I was afraid, but that I loved her too. I don't think she forgave me right away, but eventually, some normalcy of life resumed. Thankfully, that was the last time I remember her having an episode.

Even now, thinking about this, my heart hurts for mama. She had been so busy raising so many kids, and there always seemed to be kids and grandkids, and friends, and friends of friends around. The busyness in our house seemed constant. She never seemed to begrudge her life, but then she also never had the opportunity to seek healing for herself. She just continually gave of herself to everyone, until she would become tapped out. Then something would trigger that deep pain of rejection she struggled with and one of the episodes would come. Regardless, what I do know, is that she was a tower of strength and nursed my dad thru his final days on this earth.

Many years later, in her final years, she seemed to have found the peace she was lacking and would read her Bible constantly. The last night before the open-heart surgery that took her life, she was smiling and positive, knowing full well where she was headed if God called her home. I mention all of this, because thru my mother's suffering and desperation, her desire to end her life became a generational curse for me. The seed was planted when I was very young and many times, later in life, I fell into that same trap. More on that later.

4 EARLY DAYS OF MINISTRY

When I was about the age of eight, my father bought me my first piano and I started taking lessons. I learned quickly and discovered that God had blessed me with musical talent. Especially with the ability to site read music – meaning I can look at a brand, new piece of music and play it the first time. My friend, Martha, also a musician, and I would alternate playing the piano and organ together every Sunday at our home church. I also believe that God used this training time as another means to build my faith in Him.

After only a few months of taking lessons, my piano instructor decided we were going to have a recital. She handed Martha and I music to "Theme to Romeo and Juliet". She wanted us to do a duet. Martha had been playing piano much longer than I and God had blessed her with the ability to play by ear – meaning, she only needed to hear a piece of music and she would be able to play it. I on the other hand, was instantly terrified. I had only taken lessons for a few months and this was the most difficult piece I had encountered. But the people pleaser I was becoming, set out to learn it.

I practiced for hours every night. I fumbled through it many times, continually messing up, to the point of tears. One evening, after having a terrible rehearsal with Martha, when I got home, I escaped into the woods. I remember sitting in one of my favorite spots, crying my heart out that I was going to fail my teacher, my best friend, and my mom and dad. My mom had always taught me to pray when I felt low. So, I did just that. I had one of my "come to Jesus" moments, where I poured out my heart and told Him all my fears. By the time I had finished, I remember a sense of peace and I had a "knowing" that God was going to help me through this.

When I went back to the house, I asked my dad for a verse I could use to help me through this and he gave me the classic **_Philippians 4:13 I can do all things through Christ who strengthens me_**. Night after night, I sat at my piano, practicing that song, over and over and over. When I was feeling like a failure, I'd quote the verse daddy gave me and I'd press on.

Recital night came, Martha and I played our duet, and it came off without a hitch! I was thrilled and relieved it was over. But that experience reinforced my faith and taught me the power of quoting scripture – though there have been many times over the years, I've forgotten this truth, or truthfully, pushed it aside.

It was a great time in my life. After just a few months, my dad invited me to use my newfound talent in his ministry. He travelled all over Kentucky, Ohio, Virginia and West Virginia, preaching in small churches in the back country. I began to travel with him and would play the piano and lead the worship and then he would preach. Getting to spend that time with my dad was pure bliss!   It was usually just the two of us and these times with him are my favorite memories of my childhood.   He was a quiet and thoughtful man, but when he did speak, it was with such godly wisdom.   God used him to teach, preach, counsel, and heal by faith – yes, I witnessed healing miracles!

It was about this time when my oldest brother, Butch, had been diagnosed with Leukemia.   The day he got the news, he was sitting on our porch steps when dad got home from work.   I remember seeing my oldest brother, a big, muscular man, who had fought in Vietnam and wasn't afraid of any man, fall into daddy's arms crying, scared of this death sentence he had received that morning.   My dad calmly pulled a vile of oil out of his pocket, anointed Butchy's head with the oil, and quietly prayed over his son.   That was the first time I remember seeing the two of them just sit and talk for hours and it was that night that Butch gave his heart to Christ.

The following week, Butch went for a follow-up appointment. The doctors retested him and to their amazement, they found no evidence of the leukemia in his body.   Thinking they had made a mistake, they tested him again and the same results came back – no sign of the disease.   We all knew that God had healed him, and He had used my dad and his faith as the instrument for healing.

I was so proud that my dad had confidence in me to use me in his ministry.   Many times, I would get home from school in the

14

afternoon, to find my dad sitting on the porch waiting for me or even at the bus stop. I'd quickly slip a skirt on (usually over my shorts or rolled-up jeans, tom-boy that I was), and we'd head off in his truck to our next meeting. I'd often have to do my homework as he drove those few hours and mama would always have sandwiches packed for us.

As I mentioned, daddy was a quiet man, so on the occasion he felt like talking, those were the most special trips. Our talks always centered around God. I loved that even as a child, he talked to me like I was an adult and always spoke godly truth to me. Once when I was struggling with friends at school, he quietly listened to me complain about how I was being treated. Finally, he spoke up and told me, "You'll have many people call themselves "friend", but you will always know your true friends; they are the ones that will always point you back to Christ". A simple statement but packed with so much wisdom. It has stuck with me and helped me with relationships most of my life.

Again, the devil was there in the wings, waiting to snatch away all the good God was doing in my life. That same year, at the age of eight, I was again sexually abused by someone close to our family. But this time, it wasn't just once – it happened often over the next two years. He was a teenage boy. There's no need to give a name, or even the dirty details, because it's forgiven and under the blood of Christ. It's not my desire or goal to cause embarrassment or bring shame or conviction. That's the job of the

Holy Spirit.

However, that period of my life was deeply painful. I felt trapped and alone. I couldn't even tell my dad – I believed to my core that he would kill this person and I'd lose my dad forever. And I couldn't tell my mom, well because she told daddy everything! So, I kept it quiet and bore the shame and humiliation. The abuse stopped when I was ten, but the damage was done. The wounds from this sin against me, cut deep, and a darkness began to build in me. I managed to keep it pushed down for many years, but eventually it would erupt.

5 TUMULTUOUS TEENS

As a child I was not fat, but always a little pudgy. Like most adolescents, I began to develop a negative self-image and became preoccupied with my body image. My psyche was already severely broken from the abuse, and the extra weight and poor self-image just compounded the brokenness I was already struggling with. I thought I was fat – I described myself as fat - I was called fat by others around me.

The breaking point for me, was on a Sunday morning, as I walked into Sunday school class and headed towards the back where there were open seats. One of the boys, mooed like a cow as I walked past. Yes, he was inferring I was fat, like a heifer. I know to him it was a joke, but at the time, I was humiliated. Especially when everyone, including the Sunday school teacher, laughed. It only added to the darkness growing in my soul. I don't blame him – he was a kid himself and a teaser. I don't think there was evil intent on his part. I accept that it was my decision to internalize the things that were said. At the time, I didn't know how to handle it and I chose to believe the lies of the enemy and adopted those negative self-images as part of my identity.

Even though I was pudgy, I was an active kid. My parents owned a one-hundred, acre farm and I hiked a couple miles every day in the forests surrounding our home. However, we lived in the south and our normal diet was heavy in fats and fried foods and my favorite drink, Pepsi! Over the next months, I became severely distressed and depressed about my weight. Not knowing how to take healthy steps to change that, I began a regime of destruction against my body that I would fight for decades. I started by starving myself – literally denying myself all food. I'm amazed I got away with it for as long as I did.

My daily routine would be to get up, dress and hurry off to the bus, before mama had a chance to push food in me. I'd find a spot during lunch to hide from everyone at school and again, avoid eating. When I got home each afternoon, I'd get one piece of white bread and coat it with about a ¼ inch of white sugar (edge to edge) and I would slowly eat that, savoring every bite, and would eat nothing else.

I have no explanation for why I chose bread and sugar. Just that I craved both and it gave me an energy boost, if only temporary. I would then retreat to the forest (my sanctuary) with my dogs. I'd stay there, past dinner time if my parents let me get away with it. Upon returning home, my mother would push me to eat dinner, but I'd decline saying I already ate. I would then escape into my room to read and hide from the world or I would play my piano for hours. When I would travel with my dad, I would pretend like I was eating in the truck and quickly discard the evidence when we got to our destination.

I managed to keep it from my parents for a few months.

However, I eventually began to develop blisters in my mouth and throat. Most days I would have dizzy spells and felt so weak that it became a struggle to move. One day, basically the jig was up - I passed out at school. Yep, just like that – boom! I hit the floor. The school nurse, of course reported it to my parents, who then took me to the doctor. I was admitted to the hospital (which was terrifying) and after examining me, the doctor reported to my parents that I had anemia, hypoglycemia (low blood sugar) and that with the weight loss and thrush in my mouth, it appeared I had malnutrition.

The look of confusion on my parents faces, left me so ashamed. I had a lot of explaining to do. I told them I had been trying to lose weight. I accepted the fault, because it truly was mine. My mom was a busy woman – always taking care of a big group of people and as for my dad, I had never lied to him, so he took me at my word that I had eaten. It's understandable that my absence from the dinner table didn't raise alarm for them. However, from that point on, I was forced to sit at the table with them at every meal. So now, I had to find another method to keep the weight off.

I don't recall how I learned about bulimia, but it became my next tool to fight the excess pounds. To make my parents happy, I'd heartily eat my meals (to the point of binge-eating) and then I'd slip to the bathroom to purge. If the house was full of people, I'd tell my parents I was going for a walk in the woods and would purge there, as quickly as I could. I found purging was much easier than starving myself, as my body would hold onto some of the calories (it's impossible to completely purge everything). So, I had enough energy to function somewhat normally, but it would keep me from gaining weight and often found myself losing pounds.

This continued throughout the rest of my teen years and into my early twenties. If anyone near me would have known anything about that disease, the evidence was clearly visible. The scars on my knuckles, the heavy intake of food with no weight gain, and the false sense of euphoria that I would feel after purging and then would fall right back into depression. Self-hatred became a catalyst for this disease, for only with it and bulimia as my companions, could I bare to live with myself. This rollercoaster became a huge part of my life for many years. Yet another secret – what I call masks - I had learned to wear.

When I was twelve years old, during one of the revivals at our home church, several of my friends went forward to receive Christ as their Savior. At that time, I did not – I mean, I was the only one left standing in the pew. I remember seeing my dad look back at me and I'm sure he was wondering and hoping I would make a public declaration too. However, I've always had the mind of an analyst – I don't do anything or accept any "truth" just because others do. I think it through and decide in my own time what I believe and then I act.

While I fully believed in the existence of God from my earliest of memories and was working in multiple ministries, I had not made the decision to ask Christ into my heart. I certainly had no real comprehension of who the Holy Spirit really was at that point. I knew that nothing would make my dad prouder than to be able to baptize me, along with my friends that coming Sunday, but still I wasn't ready.

It was several weeks later when I had another vivid encounter with God, that I ultimately gave my heart to Christ. However, this time, I was under attack by the devil. Our farm in Kentucky was 10 miles from the nearest town. So, once the lights went out, the nights there were so black that you literally could not see your hand in front of your face. I would always try to fall asleep before daddy turned out the last light in the house. Otherwise, I'd be overcome by fear and lay awake half the night.

One night, I awoke in the middle of the night – I have no idea what time as I had no clock. I had been having one of the night terrors. I felt paralyzed and was sweating and struggling to breath as usual. I couldn't see anything in the pitch black of the night. I lay there, as quiet as I could, trying to overcome the fear I was experiencing. I didn't dare get out of bed for fear of the unknown in the dark! Mom and dad always told me to think about positive things when this would happen. I was trying my best to think about something that would stop the fear – actually, pure terror – that I was feeling.

At first, nothing helped.   Then I started thinking about my friends going forward and being baptized.   The whole question of Jesus and salvation began to swirl around in my head.   I remember distinctly praying – actually, I began to bargain with God. My prayer went something like this, "God, I know you are real – I've felt you. But I need to know that Jesus is real too.   I'm scared, and I need to know that you'll save me.   Jesus, if you're real, come and live in my heart. Save me from this fear.   Save me from this evil I feel all around me. Amen".

That little prayer was it! And you know what!?!   He did just that.   He saved me!   After that very short and simple prayer, the fear was gone – I felt the weight of it lift off me and peace flowed over me, head to foot - and I never had another night terror again! Later that week, my dad and I were traveling to one of our meetings and on the way home, I whispered to him (I'm not sure why it was a whisper – maybe because it was dark and he had been so quiet), but I whispered to him that I had given my heart to Jesus and that I wanted him to baptize me the following Sunday - and he did!

So now, you're probably thinking, awe good – she's accepted Christ, she's healed from all the ugly that happened to her years before, right!?!   Well, sorry, but that's not what happened! As I mentioned before, anytime God does something good, the devil is always nearby, ready to try to snatch it away.   Still in my youth, I had not fully realized how God can take these ugly events and turn them into good.

Gen 50:20 You meant evil against me,
but God meant it for good…

I continued to work with my dad's ministry and in several of the youth ministries in our church – the puppets and music being my favorites. I learned to stay busy so as not to think so much about what was clearly going on inside of me. There I was, just a kid, doing the Lord's work, and yet feeling so filthy and worthless inside. Even though the sins against me were not my fault, I internalized all the guilt and shame that typically goes with sexual abuse.

On top of that, I was stacking up many sins of my own. I read the Bible – I knew that my body was the temple of God and that I'm to take care of it. I guess in a twisted way I was able to justify my own sin against my body (the bulimia) by thinking I was healthier being thinner, than fatter. How we deceive ourselves! Then one day, my whole world was turned upside down, and life would never be the same.

6 MY GREATEST LOSS

Death was not a stranger to me. When I was twelve, I had lost two brothers-in-law that I adored, Mike Noren, who died of leukemia, and Steve Laws, who died in a boating accident. Around the same time, Granny died from a myriad of health issues. We lost all three of them within a few months of each other. It was particularly painful losing my brothers-in-law. However, the next time death came, it devastated me.

When I was fourteen, mama was hospitalized with back issues, and put in traction to help relieve the pain.   As my dad and I drove to the hospital one evening to visit her, he lost control of the car and we went off the road. I was terrified. My dad was always strong and in control of himself.   He got the car stopped without wrecking, but we were both shook up.

When we got to the hospital, my Aunt Chris and Uncle Jim were there visiting.   I pulled my Aunt Christine to the side and told her what happened.   She insisted that my dad let my cousin Doug, drive us home, with Uncle Jim and her following. I believe it was one of the hardest things my dad did, but he conceded.   He had become dizzy and didn't realize he had wandered off the road until it was too late.   My dad had never been sick in his life. Honestly, no one could remember him ever even having a cold.

He began to see a local doctor, who basically diagnosed him

with anxiety. Ha! He clearly didn't know my dad! The man didn't have an anxious bone in his body! But daddy, being a humble man, didn't question him and just followed the doctor's orders. Eventually, his symptoms got worse and after a few months, he went to see a doctor at the Veteran's hospital in Lexington, KY. He was diagnosed with a brain tumor. After many hours of surgery, we got the news that it was malignant. That ugly, ugly word – cancer! Oh how, I hate that word and that awful disease.

Over the next 18 months, I watched it utterly, destroy my dad. Imagine, a 6'1" tower of strength and health, broad-shouldered and muscular man, reduced to a skeleton that my mother could pick up and carry. Imagine what that does to a young, already broken mind, to see her hero reduced to a bag of bones! The roots of anger grew deeper, and this time, a great deal of it was being leveled towards God. Why was He taking my daddy away!?! I mean, I watched my dad pray and heal my brother by faith! I saw God work through him to heal many people. Why would God, not heal my dad!?! I knew daddy had the faith! I knew I had the faith – I knew God could do it! But God wasn't healing him. I just couldn't understand it. The more I thought about it, the angrier I got at God!

James 1:20 For the anger of man does not produce the righteousness of God.

On July 13, 1981, my dad went to heaven. I still vividly remember, listening to the death rattles as he lay there on his bed, and when the final breath came, I kept wishing and praying for one more – please Lord, just one more breath. But it never came, and daddy was gone.

Martha's extended family owned the funeral home. It was her dad, Tebe, who was also my dad's friend, that came to get his body. I watched as Tebe put his hand on daddy's chest and lowered his head as he sobbed – it was heart-wrenching. Tebe then loaded him into the back of the hearse and daddy left our home forever. His viewing lasted three days due to all the folks that wanted to come and pay respects. The funeral service was beautiful. Martha sang his favorite songs and we laid him to rest up on the hillside, beside his parents. Going home that day after the funeral, I was so empty inside – so utterly, empty. I had never felt so alone in my life. Not only was my daddy gone, but I no longer felt the presence of God.

Prov 13:12 Hope deferred makes the heart sick.

I would like to say that after a short period of time, I began to heal, and life was restored, but that would not be true. The first year after losing daddy, I was in such a deep state of depression, I remember my mom and older brother, Sam voiced concern. So, I got involved in music at the high school and it helped to distract me, but the pain never really subsided. I'd cry myself to sleep every night.   Martha pushed me to get involved in more activities in the church and I did, but more to make her happy than for serving God. At this point I had stopped talking to God. I was too angry at Him for taking my dad. All joy had been stripped from me. The stronghold of people-pleasing had taken hold too. I'd bury the pain and do what I had to do to make those around me not worry.   Just another mask.

From that point on in my teen years, even though I had many, really, good friends and a family I knew loved me, my life was filled with confusion and that very deep seeded anger had not only taken root, but bitterness had become firmly established in my heart.   And with that came more depression, self-hatred, self-doubt, and often overwhelming insecurities about my body and even about the way I talked!   I talk soft and sometimes fast and was teased relentlessly about this all throughout my childhood. A side note on that topic, I now understand how the enemy would use this to try to quiet me in the Lord's service.

You might say that it's normal for a teenager to have insecurities, and that's true. But in observing and talking to other teens around me (remember, I'm an analyst), I can tell you mine were much more heightened, almost to the point, I was afraid I was losing my mind.   But I remained silent – I kept pushing all the pain deep inside – I buried everything!   As a result, my whole self-image had become completely distorted. I didn't feel I could talk to anyone and being left alone in one's own mind is a dangerous thing.   I literally hated life.

Prov 8:36 Those who hate me, love death.

7 ANOTHER GOD ENCOUNTER

*Jeremiah 17:9 The heart is deceitful above all things,
and desperately sick; who can understand it?*

Then one day, God showed up. Now understand, I knew in
my mind and heart that God was always there, but our feelings are
deceiving.   In my anger and depression, I felt so alone.   I now
know that it was I who was pushing God away, but at the time, I
only understood the misery I was feeling. To get my attention, I
believe that God gave me two visions. They were so real - I
honestly felt like I was living through it right then. Each time, I
was in my bed, but I was not asleep.

*Hebrews 2:14 Therefore, since the children share in flesh and
blood, He Himself likewise also partook of the same, that
through death He might render powerless him who had the
power of death, that is, the devil.*

In the first vision, I was standing in a stark white room – I
assumed it was a hospital room.   I could see my dad laying on a
gurney. He looked pale and like a skeleton.   He was looking at
me. I started to walk towards him but stopped dead in my tracks as
the top of his head came off – it fell right to the floor.   Then, I saw
what looked like little imps or gremlins, flowing out of his head as
though it was blood flowing – hundreds of them – they just kept
coming!

Startling and confusing – right!?! Um, yeah, very much so. I didn't understand it at the time, but after many years of pondering that one, I wondered if God was telling me - in a weird way - that Satan was the agent in my dad's death. Why? Well, maybe because I was so angry and needed someone to blame and at that time, I was blaming God for taking my dad. I know that God is the author and sustainer of all life.

Acts 17:25 And he is not served by human hands, as if he needed anything. Rather, he himself gives everyone life and breath and everything else.

Acts 17:28 'For in him we live and move and have our being.' As some of your own poets have said, 'We are his offspring.'

1 Timothy 6:13 In the sight of God, who gives life to everything, and of Christ Jesus, who while testifying before Pontius Pilate made the good confession

But scripture also tells us that Satan is very much an agent of death (Hebrews 2:14 noted above). He can cause sickness and death – if God allows it, just as he did with Job's family - *Job 1:12 The LORD said to Satan, "Very well, then, everything he has is in your power, but on the man himself do not lay a finger." Then Satan went out from the presence of the LORD* – and in the case of my dad, clearly God allowed it. Still, I questioned, why?

Now, had God left me hanging with just this vision, I might have walked around even more befuddled and healing might have taken longer than ever. I know, that my dad had no demon, much less a legion of demons, in him! Again, he was the most spirit filled person I've ever known. But God's ways are higher than ours, just as His thoughts are higher than ours (*Isaiah 55:9*). By this time in my life, even though I was angry at Him, I knew enough about God's character to not question that He had a message in this vision and with time, He would give me clarity.

Revelation 21:4–5 There will be no more death or mourning or crying or pain, for the old order of things has passed away'

He who was seated on the throne said,

'I am making everything new!'

It was just a few weeks later when I had the second vision. In this vision, I was sitting on our living room couch and daddy walked in thru the front door, just like he had done most days of my life. He walked past me and headed towards the kitchen, just as he always did. I got up and followed, just like I always did. In life, he would always put his lunch pail down and then turn and hug and kiss mama first, and then me.

But this time, he didn't stop. With his lunch pail in hand, he continued out the back door, and I followed. After I got out the door, daddy turned and looked at me and put his hand up, as though to tell me to stop, which I did. He then spoke and said "Everything's ok. I'm ok. But you can't follow me this time.". He gave me a look that was filled with such peace and love. Then he turned and walked away.

At this point everything became surreal – like a mist came in and covered the image of his back as he walked away. I stood there, tears flowing as I watched him disappear. The dad that I saw in this vision was healthy, vibrant and strong, not the skin covered skeleton that we had buried and that I had seen in the first vision.

Even to this day, I'm not sure how best to explain it, but I felt God had allowed my dad to visit me in this vision, to reassure me that 1) he was indeed ok – daddy had exchanged the old, decayed flesh (first vision) for a new, healthy body and he was in heaven with God and he was happy, and 2) it was ok for me to continue living - I couldn't "follow him this time".

I knew subconsciously, I had been on the road to death myself and both my dad and God were telling me, I couldn't continue that path, and that I was going to be ok - somehow. I will admit that I did have some peace after having those visions, but the struggle was far from over. The anger and bitterness were so deeply rooted, they had become part of my identity. I wish I could tell you I had jumped off that path to death, but sadly, life continued the same as before.

At this point I was in my Junior year of high school. I was in the marching band and jazz band and continued to share the responsibility for playing piano for our church, with Martha. I do have many good memories from band and church. I loved music and what friends I allowed near me, still hold a very special place in my heart.

That year, I had my first boyfriend, Phillip, who took me to my first (and only) prom – parties are not my thing - then my first heartbreak when he dumped me for another girl. I eventually moved on and in my Senior year, began to date, Donny, who was sweet though very broken himself. That relationship too ended in disaster as well, though not before I gave up what I had left of my innocence to him. Again, I kept it secret – I wore the good-girl mask very well. But the sin heaped more shame and guilt upon the pile I was already carrying. If only I had practiced what my faith taught and had laid all of it at the foot of the cross, where Jesus had already paid for that sin and guilt. Sadly, I carried it for many more years.

8   LEAVING HOME

I graduated from high school in 1983 and went to work for a local attorney in Paintsville, for more than a year. During that time, I moved out on my own. I shared a home and split the rent with my older sister, Yvonne, but I was making my own way. After a while, I felt the pull to move to Ohio. Thinking maybe a change would be good for me, I moved to Dayton in 1985. Deep down, I knew I was just running away – another mask.

Martha was very upset with me for moving. It hurt me that she was so upset and didn't support my move. I wonder now if she realized that I was running away too. As much as I loved her, I never shared the depth of my shame with her. I would hint at things that had happened, but quickly cover it up, to make it look like all was fine and well. I think I was afraid she would think less of me if she knew all the sorted details, even though I know that wasn't her character.

I had spent so much time with her over the years, I know she detected my depression from time to time – she would comment on it but wouldn't press me to talk unless I wanted to and usually I didn't. It was really in this relationship with her, that I discovered it was easier to be the listener. It's my nature to listen, more than talk. Martha was a talker – always so free to share the deepest parts of her heart – the very same parts that I buried deep and refused to let any light shine on.

Martha was transparent and true-blue – as good a person as anyone could be, especially after she came to know God herself. In my heart, she was my sister, not just a friend. We were 20 years old at that time and I knew she was on the path to marry her true love, Barry. So, I believed it was time for me to move on too. I knew she would forgive me, which she did. It wasn't in her nature not to.

I was her maid-of-honor in her wedding. We stayed in touch and I would visit every chance I got. I never questioned or doubted Martha's love for me. Little did I know then that the world would not be blessed with her life for much longer. Her lovely life ended when we were 29 years old. At that point, next to losing my daddy, that was the most heart-wrenching experience I had ever experienced. I still miss her deeply, to this day.

9 ROARING TWENTIES

By the time I reached my twenties, there was such a dichotomy inside my head – two identities that were in complete opposition to each other, yet there they resided, together in my brain. On the one hand, I had many amazing experiences with God when I was much younger and felt my best when I was in His service. I went through periods where I enjoyed being around people who loved Him. Even though I had cut off communication with Him, I could feel Him there, tugging on my spirit to come back to Him.

On the other hand, I felt the presence of evil continually bombarding my mind. I knew then, and I know now, I was not possessed. I believed God owned my spirit, but I most definitely was being oppressed. I could put on the good girl mask and join in the Lord's work, all the while feeling complete contempt for myself and sometimes, others around me. The enemy of my soul had gotten his foot in the door and had successfully set up what felt like impenetrable, strongholds inside my mind. Little did I realize then, it would still take decades and great pains and effort, to root those out completely.

Philippians 2:12 Wherefore, my beloved, as ye have always obeyed...work out your own salvation with fear (awe) and trembling

After moving to Ohio, I lived with my oldest sister, the first year and again became involved in the music at the Abundant Life Baptist Church, which she belonged to. It was a good church and I loved the people. But again sadly, I was just going thru the motions. My service had no joy. Most of my relationships felt empty, for I really didn't trust anyone, completely. The absence of an intimate relationship with God, left me open to the enemy playing with my mind and planting seeds of distrust. Even though I was surrounded with people, I was lonely and depressed. I had somewhat mastered how to hide it.

Sometimes, I would run into someone who had discernment and would call me out. Anger and bitterness were ever present. Those who were brave enough to call me out, received the brunt of that anger and by then, a pure rage that had taken up residence. New idols began to take root; pride and haughtiness. They were just more masks I learned to wear. But those masks, I learned to wield like a weapon. Anyone who dared to confront me about anything got a taste of my wrath.

Pride and haughtiness became my shield and armor. I was fully operating in the flesh – by this time, no site of God's armor was showing in my life. Instead, I found myself pushing God, further and further to the periphery. It was also during this time, I learned that I had a gift, or rather curse, for being able to tear people to shreds with my tongue. Sadly, I took pleasure in inflicting some of the pain I felt, upon someone else. Nevertheless, the load of my pain and shame only continued to grow heavier.

During my first year in Ohio, I met Eddie. He went to our church and he quickly became my best friend. We ran around with the same group of friends and while he was strongly interested in me as more than a friend, I was a couple years older than him and hesitant to enter any kind of relationship with him beyond friendship. However, rumors and gossip were spread and sadly, believed, that there was more going on, than there was at that time. This led to discord between me and my sister.

Instead of working through the issues, I left her home in a huff and moved in with my brother, Billy Ray and my mom (who had moved to Ohio right after I graduated high school). I also left the church. So now, on top of everything else, I had a broken relationship with my oldest sister and no church family and no ministry – God was completely gone from my life.

My pride had been pricked and the indignation that anyone would entertain gossip about me, or even question my good-girl image, led to a broken relationship that took many years to mend. Sadly, the discord in my family pushed me closer to Eddie and the gossip eventually became truth. I began a sexual relationship with him. Again, all in secret (so I thought – such a liar), forever wearing the good-girl mask, and guarding it with my pride and haughtiness armor. I lived this lie for a couple of years, until I bought my first home. It became evident to all what our relationship was, when Ed immediately moved in with me.

At this point, I was working full time, and attending the local community college part time. I had started out as an English major – thinking I would be a writer. After a year, I switched to Wright State University, as a full-time Psychology major. Odd that I chose that path, right? Well, I did so as an attempt to diagnose and heal myself. I knew I was broken, but pride wouldn't allow me to reach out and get real help – I was determined to guard my secrets and heal myself.

During my studies at WSU, I became indoctrinated into the "progressive" mindset. Where I had always thought, and voted conservative, I switched to the other side. Though I pushed God out of my life – at least I tried - He was always there – trying to convict me. I became very good at ignoring Him. In fact, my life during most of that decade was in full rebellion against anything of God. I refused to go to church for any reason. My control-freak tendencies took over – I pushed away anyone who tried to control me or challenged me on any front. I had many broken relationships along the way.

Everything that I had said I believed before, I now stood against. Where I was pro-life, I became pro-choice. Where I disliked big government, I embraced tougher, more restrictive laws. I even recall saying how "sheeple" are too stupid to make their own decisions and the finite details of their lives need to be regulated, like enforcing abortion and sterilization on those on welfare. Yeah, I drank the Kool-Aid – gallons of it!

I also started acting out these beliefs in my personal life. Instead of trying to heal myself, I decided to embrace the pain and allowed it to influence most of the decisions I made during that time in my life. After another couple years of school, I decided to switch majors again. Instead of continuing as a Psych major, I switched to pre-law and Political Science, with my associates in Psych. I didn't feel that studying Psychology was going to heal me overall. I tried applying some of the principals, but nothing seemed to help.

I had decided my destiny was in practicing law and eventually wanted to become a judge and then wrap up my career as a professor in some prestigious law school (lofty dreams, eh!?!). I convinced myself that I could affect real change in any one of those positions in society, and not the kind of change God or my parents would have been proud of. After all, I now had this rage inside of me, driving me forward. I certainly had the mouth for it – I could argue anyone under the table. Actually - it was more like I could beat them into submission with my tongue.

As I look back today, one of my greatest shames is the stance I took on pro-choice. I protested at rally's when the abortion laws were under scrutiny. I even apprenticed for a Democrat state Rep in Columbus, Ohio, who was working on bills in support of pro-choice. I wanted to be there, amongst all the action, fighting for women's rights. I thought I was going to correct all the wrongs done to women and children via the law (oxy-moron if there ever was one), since God had failed me and others, so desperately.   I was well on the path of becoming my own god!

One morning, I woke up feeling really, sick. After a while, it passed.   But then the next morning, I woke up sick again. Reality set in and I realized, I had missed a monthly cycle.   A quick trip to the doctor's office confirmed I was pregnant. I was stunned at first. After all, I was on the pill and I hadn't missed any doses. Little did I know at that time, that anti-biotics make birth control ineffective and I had just finished a round a few weeks before for sinus infection.   I remember thinking, what an inconvenience! I can't do this! I still have school to finish! I can't be a mom! I don't want kids! I never wanted kids! I swore I would NEVER have kids! I'm not having this!!!!

A few days later, I ended the pregnancy. Eddie was in full agreement, after all he was clear that he didn't want kids either. I justified it in my mind that this is my life – I have the right to choose for myself, don't I?   After all, it was just a blob of tissue, right!?!   I can tell you with certainty, that my heart grew so cold. At this point in my life, my education and future career was all that mattered to me.

Over the next year, life went on. I had quit work and was doing my studies full-time, plus some. I was carrying extra classes each quarter and was prepping for the LSAT and was trying to decide where I wanted to apply to law school. I was loving it! I had found a new identity – success was on the horizon. I could almost taste it.

Then one morning, I woke up sick – a very familiar kind of sick. I was still on the pill. I checked to make sure I hadn't missed any doses, which I hadn't. I decided I'd spare myself the cost of a doctor's appointment and picked up a pregnancy test. I was surprised to discover that I again was pregnant. Without giving it much thought, a few days later, Eddie and I again made the trip to the clinic and ended the pregnancy. It was as though I was going for a routine checkup with my doctor. No shame - no guilt - no care.

I wish I could tell you that I had felt some emotion. But the reality was, that my heart was so hardened, I felt nothing. I just went through the motions. My goals and my career plan were all that were important to me. I wasn't going to let anything get in my way. After all, the God I had known, was just a whisper in my past, for by this point, I was now my own god.

I read a post online recently by DC McAllister. She stated, "At the root of the abortion hysteria is women's unhinged desire for irresponsible sex. Sex is their god. Abortion is their sacrament. It's abhorrent as women have flung themselves from the heights of being the world's civilizing force to the muck and mire of dehumanizing depravity.". I hate to admit, but this really sums up the state that I was in at that point in my life. I was depraved to the core. I proved to myself that humans are capable of anything. Occasionally, a Bible verse I had read years before would pop in my head. One from ***Revelations 2:5 Look how far you have fallen! Turn back to me and do the works you did at first. If you don't repent, I will come and remove your lampstand from its place among the churches.*** Though my heart had grown so hard and cold, I knew that this was God trying to get thru to me. Even though I had pushed Him so far out of my life, I knew it was Him trying to call me back. Fallen I was, and from great heights.

I began having emotional melt-downs – very much like my mama had when I was a child. I would be going along just fine and then suddenly; this overwhelming rage would erupt from me like Mount Vesuvius was blowing its top. Pity the person closest to me that encountered my wrath! Many times, there was no apparent trigger. Other times, it would be stress of school or work or relationships that would take me to the ledge, ready to jump off. I remember many times, wishing I could just be done – I just wanted life to be over. I was too cowardly to end my life, but I think if I just wished for it hard enough, maybe it would just come true. The spirit of death was still hanging over my life. Deep down, I believed that I was doomed.

I began waking up in the middle of the night having panic attacks. Many times, Ed would find me in a heap in the bathroom or living room floor, hysterical and uncontrollable. I had developed a good report with one of my Psych professors, so I went to talk with him. He basically said I was having an emotional breakdown and suggested a doctor he wanted me to see. But in my pride, I refused. I still believed I could heal myself.

Looking back now, I know that this was God working on me – trying to break through the hardness in my heart. I know He had to let me come to the end of myself – to hit rock bottom – so that I would again look up to Him. But I was so full of pride, and that consuming rage that just spurred me on. My will was (and still is) very strong. I had set my will against the Almighty's. I was very much on the throne of my life. These attacks went on for the better part of a year. The more anxiety I felt, the more I threw myself into my schooling.

Then one morning, I was sick again. A trip to the doctor confirmed that I was pregnant. I remember going home and curling up on my couch, just confused. I couldn't believe that it happened again. I wasn't irresponsible – I was diligent about taking my birth control. I can't tell you I had a heart change just yet, but for whatever reason, I just did not consider abortion as an option this time.

I didn't say anything to Ed for three weeks. I just decided I would have the kid. Then one day, I was visiting my mom and blurted out to her that I was pregnant. She was very upset with me, only because Ed and I weren't married. I think it opened old wounds in her – the rejection she had suffered as a kid who was the product of premarital sex. Even though my heart was hard, hurting my mom was not something I wanted to do. So that evening, I told Ed about the pregnancy and that I intended to have the baby. He had been asking me to marry him for the past couple of years, but I had continually put him off, saying I wasn't ready. This time he asked me again, and I agreed. I knew deep inside, the only reason I was marrying him was for my mother's sake (people pleasing) and for the kid. I didn't want the child to be born without its' father. I knew then that this was not a good basis for marriage. God was no part of the decision – at least in my mind.

Two weeks later, on May 30, 1990, we were married. It was a quickly planned and simple ceremony that took place in the home of one of my sisters on a rainy day. The weather matched the depressed, state I was in that day. The only thing godly about it was the man who married us, my dad's closest friend, Wendel Gibbs. He was the man who led my dad to Christ. I think I felt him performing the ceremony would be like having part of daddy there. But it just wasn't the same. Yet, I did feel my dad there, in my mind, saying "you have doubts, don't do this!".

I've heard and seen many weddings over the years where the brides were so joyful and filled with excitement and expectations. Sadly, I was just going through the motions. We had quite a large crowd turn out on short notice. I honestly remembered thinking, "I can't wait until this day is over!". Not a great start, right!?!

It was only after the first couple months of marriage that I learned of Ed's infidelities. I had trusted him and cared very much for him. He was my closest friend - so I thought. But now I learned, he betrayed me. The betrayal, along with the hormonal imbalance from the pregnancy, sent my already heightened emotional state into a tail-spin. The rage that I had always been able to keep mostly beneath the surface, erupted in full force. I had never been a violent person, but Mr. Ed could have met his end that day, as I lobbed every heavy object, I could get my hands on, towards his head. Lucky for him, he was able to duck and avoid a direct blow.

The feelings of anger and wanting to hurt someone, became a part of the norm for quite a while. There were weeks of angry episodes (not a good way to carry a child), trying to decide whether to end the marriage then or try to recover and carry on. Maybe if I could have just had a good sob, but crying was not allowed – I refused to give in to that emotion. At that point, forgiveness was not even on the table. It was just a decision of whether to let him stay or kick his hind-end out.

Over the next few months, things calmed down inside me. I suppressed the anger and concentrated on school and getting ready for the birth of my son. Trust never really returned in our relationship. We lived with an air of suspicion hanging over us. It was not a good way to live. Pregnant and depressed, I honestly was about as miserable as a person can be. I cut myself off from most everyone in my family, except my mom, a niece, and occasionally a couple of my sisters. Slowly Eddie and I resumed a tenuous relationship.

On January 6, 1991, my sweet Aaron was born. When the doctor laid him on my chest and I looked at his beautiful face, the crustiness around my heart began to break.

Before this moment, the best way to describe what was going on inside me is a scene from Ghostbusters 2. In it there was a river of pink slime that was flowing underground, and it eventually rose up and created a shell around the museum where the evil spirit dwelled. The river of slime is analogous to the rebellion and rage that was flowing all throughout me. It became the impenetrable shell around my heart and soul (i.e. my mind, will and emotions).

The birth of my son created a fracture in the crust, though a small one. My heart swelled up with love for my boy. As I laid there, holding him, I talked to God for the first time in years. Well, it was a brief conversation – but I did thank him for my healthy, baby boy.

The first few months of the baby's life, my focus was on him and on continuing my education. As Aaron grew, I thoroughly enjoyed spending time with him. He was funny and mischievous and loved to laugh. But there was something different about Aaron as well – something that I wouldn't understand the depth of until he was almost an adult. Aaron has Asperger's – high functioning autism. We didn't have a name for it back then – at least the doctors we saw, didn't seem to know. But he was still my boy and I was enjoying the time with him. Ed seemed to enjoy fatherhood for a while – at least until the novelty wore off and it became real work. Our relationship was strained as the suspicion never lifted. And the older Aaron got and the more challenging he became, the more I saw Ed withdraw and even began to resent our son.

By the time Aaron's first birthday rolled around, I was confronted with another revelation of Ed's continued infidelity. This part of my life became like a bad scene from a terrible movie, that just kept playing over and over. I'd find out about his infidelity, he'd beg and grovel for forgiveness, I'd get a bouquet of flowers, and for the sake of my son and my mom – I'd try to put it aside and move on. Only it would be just a matter of weeks before I'd end up living through yet another episode of the same.

I tried to play the good wife – yet another mask. I think it was easier to keep it all hushed and appear normal than to continually live out the humiliation that his affairs brought me. We were struggling financially. Since having the baby, I had to reduce the number of hours I took each quarter, so I still had a couple of years of school left to finish and I didn't have a job myself. The expense of a child was putting even more strain on the marriage.

About the time Aaron was about 15 months old, I again woke

one morning feeling very ill. I was pregnant. This time I was devastated. I was in the pit again. The deep, dark, depression enveloped me. When I told Ed of the pregnancy, it was clear, he didn't want the baby. But this time, the thought of ending the pregnancy tore at my heart. I had experienced motherhood and loved my son. How could I possibly go through with another abortion!?!

Ed was insistent that he wanted to end it, to the point that he threatened to leave. We were struggling to feed the child we already had, and on the verge of losing our home. We just couldn't see how we'd make it with another. So, I caved in (yes, still very self-centered myself and ultimately my decision) and I found myself again at the clinic. But this time it was different. Where before I had felt nothing, this time, I felt like my whole insides were going to explode. My heart ached unlike anything I had experienced before. I tried to talk myself and Ed out of it while we were in the waiting room, but he insisted this was for the best.

When the doctor began the procedure, I began to shake. After a couple of minutes, I asked them to stop, but by then he said it was too late. I hated myself for what I was doing. When they finished, I was still shaking -uncontrollably. They left me there, in that room on that cold table, completely alone. It all felt surreal. I felt despicable – unworthy of life myself. I remember begging God to just take me – right then and there. I deserved death and hell! But He was silent. Instead, I believe it was God who put the face of my little boy in my mind and I knew I had to pull it together for him. Nevertheless, the weight of my sin had come bearing down on my soul.

Matthew 23:27-28 Woe to you, teachers of the law and Pharisees, you hypocrites! You are like whitewashed tombs, which look beautiful on the outside but on the inside are full of the bones of the dead and everything unclean. [28]In the same way, on the outside you appear to people as righteous but on the inside, you are full of hypocrisy and wickedness.

The following weeks were extremely painful. Mentally and emotionally I was falling apart, and this was just the beginning. I struggled with more emotional melt-downs, all the while, wishing for death. I began to isolate myself from everyone. I also began having insomnia. I couldn't even stand to look at myself in the mirror. I remember once, I woke up in the middle of the night. I walked into the bathroom to splash some water on my face. As soon as I looked up at myself in the mirror, I was completely repulsed to the point of nausea, by the stranger I saw looking back and I crumbled.

Sleep deprivation, depression, anxiety attacks, studying for school, fractured marriage pitted with betrayal, broken family relationships, financially broke, and a toddler - not a good mix! The weight of all my past and current failures left me little hope for the future. The only thing that spurred me on and kept me somewhat sane, was my son and the thought that I might still be able to have some part of the career I had dreamed about.

I had mastered wearing the mask of normalcy when I was in public. I was consumed with fear that people would find out about all the evil in my heart (at least I recognized it for what it was). I think those that I allowed close to me had a sense that something was terribly wrong, but probably couldn't have imagined the depth of the despair and depravity I had willingly walked into.

As most who hide sin, I became a great judge of other's sin. It was nothing for me to get on my pedestal and rail on about someone else's sin. Pride and haughtiness were still very much my armor and rage, was my arsenal. All my secrets were buried, but my emotions were in such a volatile state, I felt like the dam that was holding back the flood was on the verge of breaking.

I continued to pour myself into my school work. My mom would watch Aaron while I went to school. Each night, I would put him to bed, and I would stay up studying into the wee hours of the morning. Studying and chasing my toddler were distractions for a while.

I also started working out and riding my bike again, with Aaron on the back, obsessively, every day. The only joy I felt was in the life of my boy, and the freedom I felt when I felt the wind blowing against me, as I rode my 10-speed along the bike trail. And I had lost quite a bit of weight, finally. Life continued this way for the next 11 months. Financially, we were on the verge of collapse and I was emotionally a basket-case, but my pride still wouldn't allow me to reach out for help.

Then one morning, as I was waking, I rolled over onto my stomach and felt a knot in my belly. My first thought was, "this is either a tumor, or I have a baby in my belly". I hadn't missed my period (well, it had been spotty), but I truly did not expect to be pregnant. So, I went to the doctor, fully expecting him to find a tumor. But no, it was a baby and, I was already four months into the pregnancy! Thank God, there was no question in my heart or mind as to whether I would have this baby. I didn't care whether Ed was happy about it or not – didn't even ask him. I just knew that never again would I ever end the life of a child.

Our plan had been to move to New Mexico, which is where I wanted to go to law school. We had already packed up as much as we could, anticipating the move in the coming months. But with a second child on the way, I knew that my dreams of law school had ended – it was no longer an option. I think I could have pulled it off with one kid. But certainly not with two little ones and not that far from home. Especially not with a husband who was prone to infidelity.

I was a few months away from getting my bachelor's degree, but fearing that Ed would leave, I found myself a part-time job in a bridal shop and determined that my kids and I would make it, somehow. I truly believed the expense of the new childbirth would push him over the edge. But he didn't leave - at least not physically. In December of 1993, I finally got my degrees; BA in Liberal Arts, Political Science (pre-law) and associates in Psychology (lacked 15 hours having my 2nd BS in Psych). I was relieved to be done. My family relationships were so fractured (my fault as I had pushed everyone away), that I refused to walk in the graduation ceremony. I truly believed none of my siblings would attend, so what was the use! So, that accomplishment went quietly by the way. I kept telling myself, I'd eventually finish up the 15 hours I had left on the Psych BS, but I was burned out and I never returned to school.

The following March 23, 1994, my precious little girl, Autumn, was born. As I held that perfect little creature the first time, in my heart and mind, I dedicated both her and her brother to God. Despite all the hateful things I had done and even said to Him, He gave me these two perfect little lives. I felt so undeserving, but at the same time, I was so thankful to have them.

I have a picture of me holding Aaron, as he was holding his new baby sister, when she was just a few hours old. The first time

I looked at that picture, I knew in my spirit that it would just be the three of us, and for the first time, I was ok with that. The love that I was feeling for these two little creatures, was creating more fissures in that crust around my heart. Believe me, it was far from breaking off, but the process had begun.

As we brought Autumn home from the hospital, Ed warmed up to her and took way more interest in her than he ever did Aaron. She had such a sweet personality, right from the beginning. She equally loved me and her daddy. For a moment, I thought we might make it as a family unit. Over time, Ed returned to his philandering and the affairs continued. But by then, I didn't really care. He was just a source of income I needed to take care of our children.

After Autumn and the revelation of yet another affair, the marital affection ended. I didn't want him to touch me, knowing he was spending time with someone else and I didn't want to risk getting pregnant by him again, with things as they were. Divorce wasn't in the cards for me – at least I did not want to initiate it. When Autumn had just turned one year old, I had started working in the IT department of a local mechanical parts, distribution company. The new income was a huge relief. I thought it would ease a lot of the stress in the marriage, but it didn't.

It was around this same time when my friend, Martha, had become very sick. Her liver had become diseased. They had taken her to the University hospital in Columbus, Ohio, which was just an hour away from where I lived. So as often as I could, I would travel there and spend as much time with her as possible. She had been in a coma for periods of time, while in the hospital. After she came out of that, she started to get better. Her liver enzymes had improved, and we had hope that she would be ok. They even let her go home after many weeks in the hospital.

After six months of struggling with the disease, in November of 1995, she developed pneumonia and in her weakened state, she lost the fight and went home to be with Jesus. I was devastated. Knowing how good a person Martha was, and how evil a person I had been, it just made no sense to me. Why would God take her and leave me alive!?! This added to the depression I was already fighting and believe me, so much confusion in my mind. What kind of God was He anyway!?!

10   THE END AND A NEW BEGINNING

The following January, I decided to sell my home. It was a mobile home, sitting in a really, nice community – cheap living for a college student. But I was able to sell it for three times what I had paid for it. Ed and I had done a lot of work on it before the kids were born, so it was in good condition. I didn't realize it at the time, but that whole process, was a God thing.   He knew exactly what was going to happen and exactly what the kids and I would need. If only I had trusted Him sooner.

I found a house, two blocks from my mother's home and it was empty and ready for us to move in.   I had intentionally looked in the area near my mom, so that I could be near her to help her as needed.   She was 70 years old at the time and her heart was not healthy.   The money I made on the sale of the old home, was all I had as down payment on the new home. With my new job and good income, we easily were approved for the loan.

Although things were looking up on the financial side, it was still quite a stressful time, as I had to manage all of it on my own, while working full-time and being the primary caretaker of both kids. Ed had pretty much excused himself from making any decisions.   In just a few short weeks I sold our old home and we moved into the new one.

Sadly, it was just five weeks later when my mother had open heart surgery and within 24 hours of the surgery, we lost her as well. Again, I was devastated from the loss of my mom. Even though I was 31 years old, I felt completely orphaned. It is such a strange feeling to know both of your parents are gone – that you can never talk to them or hug them again. The ever-present depression grew even deeper. I had lost my best friend and now my mom – what else could possibly go wrong!?! My advice – never ask that question!

Aaron was a challenging, and emotional kid. I'm not surprised with the nervous and emotional state I was in most of his young life (including the time I was pregnant with him). Then on top of that, Ed's abusiveness towards him. Let me clarify, I have no problem disciplining a child, but what Ed did was abuse and I would not stand by and allow that to happen to my kids. So, the relationship was very volatile. At this point, I worked days and Ed worked nights, managing a pizza place. It was good in that we didn't have to pay for daycare for two kids, but I had a sense that things were not good for Aaron while I was away.

After only a couple of months, one day I had such an overwhelming feeling of dread, I felt the need to go home at 2pm in the afternoon, to check on things. As I approached the front door, I heard Autumn screaming and crying. She was such a sweet kid, but when she got emotional – whoo! – she was loud! As I unlocked and opened the door, I heard a thud coming from the back of the house. I found both my kids in the kitchen, and Aaron was laying on the floor, and now both kids were howling. Aaron had been climbing up on the counter, trying to get his sister some food. When he heard me coming in the door, he thought it was his dad and panicked. As he tried to climb down, he fell to the floor, which was the thud I heard. I discovered they had not been fed all day. Both kids were still in their jammies, Autumn's diaper was completely saturated, and both kids were traumatized.

I calmed them, got them cleaned up and fed, and then went upstairs and found Ed, dead asleep and wreaking of liquor. Trust me, I didn't leave him that way. I ripped the covers off him, pushed him off the bed, and cussed him a blue streak. We had an extremely heated fight that day. The next morning, I took my kids and enrolled them in a Christian daycare. I never allowed Ed to be alone with them again, and he never seemed to mind. We never even saw him much after that— he would be gone to work by the time we got home and asleep (usually on the couch) when we left the next morning. So, the only interaction any of us had with him was a few hours on the weekend.

I had made peace with the belief that he would eventually leave, and he did. It was just a month later, when we had yet another huge fight over his abusiveness towards Aaron and then this time, towards Autumn too. During this episode, Ed had already struck Autumn really, hard in anger, and his hand was raised, ready to hit Aaron, and usually when he started on him, he didn't stop easily. So, I stepped in between them, and he turned his rage on me. I had already warned him never to hit me – he likely would not have survived if he had. That hot July night, in 1996, Ed went to work and never came home again. Aaron was 5 years old and Autumn was 2 years old at the time.

A week later, things went from bad to worse. I had only been working a little over a year when the company decided to downsize. Since I was the most recent hire, I was the first to be laid off. That old familiar spirit of death quickly settled on me again. Feeling humiliated and defeated, I found myself wishing for death as I sat in my car, completely overwhelmed. All sources of income were gone, and I had two little lives depending on me. Ed was gone – hadn't heard from him for days. I knew that he wouldn't help. I honestly sat there trying to think of the best place to drive my car into a utility pole, just to end the misery and believing my kids would be better off without me. Pitiful, right!?! But then I figured with my luck, I'd end up a vegetable and stuck in my own head forever – now THAT would be hell!

The wind had been completely knocked out of me. My best friend was gone, my mom was gone, my husband was gone, my job was gone! And I had pushed God so far out of my life, He was gone! My whole support system was completely gone from beneath me. As I sat there in my self-pity, tears began to flow. I hated crying – refused to allow myself to cry, but this time, there was no stopping it. And then there was the thought of God again. Was He still there!?! Would He do anything to help me after ALL I had done to Him!?!

Psalm 61:2 From the end of the earth I call to You when my heart is faint; Lead me to the rock that is higher than I.

My pride was strong, and it was one of the hardest things I did that day – to acknowledge my weakness and humble myself and ask for God's help. Through the tears, I prayed. "God, I don't deserve anything but death and the hottest part of hell!   But you gave me those two little creatures and a love for them, that I can't explain. Please forgive me for everything I've done to cause harm to my family and to You. Not for me, but for them, please help us!"

Through my tears, I drove to the daycare and picked up my little ones. I told them they wouldn't be coming back for a while, so they said their good-byes to the workers and their little friends and we went home. I cried a lot that night. I know the kids had to be confused.   In all my hysterical moments in the past, they had never seen tears coming from me. Plenty of hysteria, but no tears. As I held them in my arms that night, I had no idea how we were going to make it. Did God hear my prayer? Had I been so bad that He turned me over to a reprobate mind!?! Was I lost forever!?! Would my babies suffer because of all the evil I had done!?! So many thoughts went through my head.

Psalms 30:5b Weeping may tarry for the night,
but joy comes with the morning.

I have no idea what time I finally drifted off to sleep, but the next morning, as soon as my feet hit the floor, I had a new revelation! You see, the week since Ed had left, my kids were suffering with separation anxiety. Every day as I dropped them at the daycare, the ladies would have to peel them off me, so I could leave. They would cry for me, hysterically, every day. The first couple of days, they told me, little Autumn just wept all day long. It was heart-wrenching, leaving them each day. Their dad had left and wasn't coming back, and now they were afraid each time I left, that I wouldn't come back. Yet that day, the morning after I lost my job, I didn't have to leave them! My kids needed their mommy – to be right there, present while they adjusted to this new life.

I had no idea how I would financially make it – now with a much larger mortgage, no job and two little mouths to feed, but they had me. As much as I hated myself, I knew I loved them. I determined in my heart and mind that morning, that I would do whatever it took, to keep them safe and loved, and I would fight anyone who tried to hurt them.

In this revelation, I knew in my heart that as hard as I had pushed Him away, God had not abandoned me. It was I who had abandoned Him. Regardless of my rebellion and rejection of all things Christ, God was always there - a faint whisper in the back of my mind, calling me back to Him. Just as He had reached down from Heaven and marked my life at the age of three, He was reaching His hand down to me again, the prodigal, welcoming me back. I knew He had orchestrated all of this, not only for the sake of my kids, but for me as well.

That first week after I lost my job, I gave my kids, my whole attention. Laughter returned to our home and my son, who had been such a challenge, had a new calm that settled over him. I didn't realize it at the time (duh – with all the Psych studies!), even though I tried to protect him from the abusiveness, both it and the discord in the marriage were a huge part of the emotional outbursts Aaron would display.

On the other hand, Autumn fell into a bit of a depression. It's hard to imagine a two-year old depressed, but she clearly felt the loss of her daddy; a sadness had settled on her. She has always had a wisdom beyond her years. One day, a few months after Ed had left, I was talking with someone about the whole situation and clearly my anger towards him was rolling off my tongue. Autumn was sitting on the floor in front of me...I thought she was watching a cartoon. But apparently, she was listening to me and turned and said, "But, I love my daddy too". That sweet face and those simple, pain-filled words silenced me. From that point on, I never spoke in anger about their dad. It made me more determined to help my babies heal.

While divorce was not something I wanted, I knew I had to take steps to force Ed to help me financially, at least until I found another job. So, with the little I had in savings, I found an attorney and initiated court processes to get child support. Over the next few weeks, it became clear that Ed had no intentions of ever returning. I discovered he had left me for someone else and was engrossed in his new relationship. So, the separation became a dissolution process.

He never came to see his kids again. He was just gone. As I write this, it's been 22 years since he left, and he has never come back, just to see his kids. His mother, Taeko, a sweet little Japanese woman, was a huge support to me and the kids during those first few months. I was shocked – I truly did not expect her to stand with me during the process, but she did. As she said to me, "I did not raise my son to behave like this and to abandon his wife and children". I made sure that she got to see the kids however often she wanted to. During this time, she was fighting cancer, and it was just a few months later when we lost her as well. She died the following January 1997.

From July, thru October of 1996, I was without a job and things got tough as I tried to hang on to the house and provide for my kids. But what I can tell you, without doubt or hesitation, is that God supplied ALL our needs. He used people like Taeko, my brother Keith (who paid my mortgage one month), a local church, and a couple of my siblings that stepped up to help as they could. The time off, allowed me to be present, to help my kids begin to heal.

In October, I started working for Evenflo, in IT, as a Senior Systems Analyst, and my kids returned to the daycare much more at peace. A week after I started the new job, our final dissolution hearing was scheduled. Ed was a no-show, so I was awarded full custody of the kids. He was granted his visitation time, but not once did he come to see them. That same week, I also started attending Bethel Missionary Church in Xenia, with my brother, Keith and his wife, Carol, and my sister, Paulette and my kids. I was on a new journey back to God and while my heart was still very hard, I had a small amount of hope that God might still have a plan for my life.

Philippians 3:14 "Forgetting what is behind

and reaching forward to what is ahead."

I had begun reading and studying my Bible again – in the beginning, it was off and on. Like many people who sit in church pews every Sunday, I had one foot in heaven and the other, still firmly planted in hell (metaphorically speaking). Living the Christian life on Sunday but raising hell during the week! It was hard to read the words of God, knowing what I had done. The conviction was almost too much to bear at times. I still had a lot of unconfessed sin in my heart and still so much pain from all that had been done to me and all that I had done. I heard Joyce Meyer say, "Getting hurt, really hurts, but oddly, getting well, really hurts too.". That is so true!

Hebrews 4:12 For the word of God is alive and active. Sharper than any double-edged sword, it penetrates even to dividing soul and spirit, joints and marrow; it judges the thoughts and attitudes of the heart.

God's Word reveals ALL. There was no hiding when He began to expose the ugly depths of my heart and soul. I truly felt like He was performing a surgery on me. It hurt to the core. And I didn't make it any easier on myself – at first, I fought it! I was expert at justifying all my sin, after all, didn't God turn His back on me, while others abused me!?! He's omniscient and omni-present, so that means He was there and had to have seen what was done to me, right!?! Believe me, in my depravity, I was giving it right back to Him! I wanted to be free, but I had so much rage in me, that the thought of truly being free was scary. I had gotten so comfortable with that ugly decay in my heart. It was familiar and at first, I didn't really want to lose it. It was what was protecting me – you know, the pride and haughtiness were my armor, and rage was my sword!

The kids and I were finding our new normal. In the beginning, I was consumed with fear. Most days I would find myself repeatedly quoting *Deuteronomy 31:6 Fear not, nor be afraid of them: for the LORD thy God, he it is that doth go with thee; he will not fail thee, nor forsake thee.* I'd go to sleep at night saying this verse over and over in my head, and I'd wake up the next morning, only to repeat the process. I had enrolled Aaron in

Dayton Christian School and Autumn was still going to the Christian daycare. Even though I was still in a somewhat, rebellious state, it gave me peace, knowing my kids were surrounded with God's Word throughout their days.

Dating was not something I really wanted to pursue at that point. I was being pressured by a friend at work, an older lady, who for some baffling reason took a liking to me and decided she wanted me to be her daughter-in-law (oh boy, if she only knew!). So, I agreed to meet her son for dinner one night. After all, at this point, it had been almost a year since I found myself on my own.

Her son was handsome and I'm sure he was a fine person, but it became extremely apparent to me that I was NOT ready to walk that path. Throughout the whole dinner, all I did was sit there and pick out all the similarities between him and my ex-husband. As the dinner ended, I practically ran to my car to escape as quick as I could.

As I drove home that evening, I knew that with my brokenness I wasn't fit to walk into a relationship with anyone. With all the turmoil in me and the rage towards men, or really, the rage towards life, at the time, I would have pulverized any potential relationships. Besides that, sex seemed to be the theme of the day – it's what every man I met expected. Yet it was what caused me so much pain over my entire life. I decided for the first time, that I would seek healing from the true source and that source was NOT me. I also made a pledge of purity to God – for as long as I am single, I will abstain from sexual impurity.   So, until God tells me otherwise, I decided dating was not an option.   I began to pray regularly, asking for God to help me.

Romans 12:1 I appeal to you therefore, brothers, by the mercies of God, to present your bodies as a living sacrifice, holy and acceptable to God, which is your spiritual worship.
2 Do not be conformed to this world, but be transformed by the renewal of your mind…

11 THE BREAKING BEGINS

As time marched on, I began reading my Bible daily, and had picked up a few Christian books that I thought might help as well. God is faithful to answer our prayers. And sometimes, He moves at the most unexpected times. The memory of my past had never left me, but I had mastered burying it deep.   When God begins the breaking process, He goes deep.   At the time, my work offices were roughly an hour drive from my home in Dayton, each way.   I love to drive, so I found it relaxing and spent that time in deep thought and often would pray about the events of the day. Especially in the evening – I didn't like carrying my stress of the job home to my kids.

One evening as I was driving down interstate 75 towards Dayton, God opened the floodgates of my mind. Every memory of what had been done to me, and all those horrific sins I had committed, came pouring into my brain like flashes from one of those old-time movies, flickering in my mind's eye. It was overwhelming.   It was then that I had a vision. I saw a young woman walking towards me and in her arms, she held a very small baby. I recognized the woman; it was my mom. But a much younger version of my mother. At this point she had been dead almost a year. I knew the child she was carrying was mine and it looked right at me. I started crying and hyperventilating, as I was driving 65 mph down the highway.   Not a good place to be having a panic attack! The tears flowed so heavy that I eventually had to pull the car off the highway.

That vision broke me, and I knew I couldn't run from the past anymore. I had never considered what it would feel like to know that my parents would know my deepest, darkest, sins. I still cringe at the thought of my dad knowing! Yet here God allowed me to see my mom, with one of the babies, whose life I ended. As *1 Timothy 1:15 reads, Christ Jesus came into the world to save sinners--of whom I am the worst* – I knew then that I was the chief among sinners. I felt the convicting power of the Holy Spirit fall on me in that car, sitting on the side of the highway, and I knew that God was offering me a chance and I believe in my heart, that it was my last chance.

I had a sense of urgency that came over me. I've since learned that's how the Holy Spirit moves on me, when He's looking to do something in my life. All I had to do was yield my will to His. As I sat there in that car, stunned, I finally acknowledged that I needed Him desperately to walk me thru the healing process. I began by asking for forgiveness and making the choice that I wanted to be free. And so, the real work began.

12 THE AWAKENING

I found myself hungry for God's Word. Each night, I enjoyed
my time with my kids, but after I put them to bed, I'd go into my
bedroom and sit, either on my bed or on the floor, with my Bible,
notebooks and any other Christian literature I could find,
surrounding me. I dug into the Word – I would read and study
and take notes for hours. I was sharing my nightly routine with a
couple of co-workers. One of them laughed and said, "Girl, you
need to get a life!". But the second one, quietly responded,
"Sounds like your life begins when you close your door each
night!". I remembered what my dad had said how to judge
friendship. This fellow, Geoff Banwart, and his wife, Rose, whom
he introduced me to a short time later, became treasured friends.

A few months later, Rose invited me to go to a women's
conference with her. I happily agreed as I wanted to spend time
getting to know her. So, we went to a little church, in a little town
north of Dayton. The music was amazing, and the message was
powerful! It was the first time I had heard a woman speaker (I
hadn't yet discovered Joyce Meyer or Beth Moore). It was clear
that God was present. But it was during the prayer time at the end
of the service that I had an encounter with Him that changed
everything for me.

I was still struggling with depression. All the ugly stuff from
my past was still part of my identity and I didn't believe that God

could, or would, ever use me for anything – I thought I had gone too far. The thought of being called into ministry was the farthest thing from my mind. I was just hoping to find forgiveness, peace and healing. I would have been happy with that. However, God revealed to me that night that He had other plans.

One of the women approached me – I had seen her eyeing me for a while and at first, it made me uncomfortable. She laid her hands on me and began to pray. I was a bit shocked – I hadn't ever experienced a service full of just women, who were so free to worship as these women were. As she prayed for me, she said the words, "and we baptize you in the Holy Spirit" and in that same moment, I heard God speak to me, as clear as if He was standing right in front of me. He told me, "You are going to teach My Word". Quite honestly, I chuckled out loud. I couldn't believe that God would give me an assignment when I was such a mess. But in that moment, with a new peace in my heart, all I could do was say "Yes" and I surrendered my life back to His service.

I felt a new sense of God moving in me after that night – my spirit had become awakened with His Spirit – a new revelation of His HOLY Spirit. I knew God – I had encountered Him as a child. I knew Jesus - I too had sought Him as a teenager and was pursuing Him again. Now, I knew I had to better understand who the Holy Spirit is. I admit, I really didn't understand who He was. I had heard about the trinity my whole life and read about Him in the Word, but never fully understood how the Holy Spirit operated.

But now I was determined to seek and understand not only who the Father, Son and Holy Spirit truly were, but also, who I was to Him.

Ephesians 1:13 - 1413 In him you also, when you heard the word of truth, the gospel of your salvation, and believed in him, were sealed with the promised Holy Spirit, 14 who is the guarantee of our inheritance until we acquire possession of it, to the praise of his glory.

Reading God's Word was (and still is) a priority, but I had also been reading other Christian books. There were three that had a major impact in my healing and growth. The first was "Risky Living – Keys to Inner Healing" by Jamie Buckingham, which Rose had recommended to me. The second was "The Three Battlegrounds" by Francis Frangipane. The third was "Shattering Your Strongholds" by Liberty Savard. I highly recommend these books to anyone who is looking for additional help in overcoming your past. As I always advise when I recommend a book, pray ahead and ask God to reveal His truth and as *1 John 4:1* instructs, test all spirits to make sure anything revealed in the literature, is from the true God. Hence, our need to know the scripture, as that, along with prayer, are our tools for discerning spirits.

As I was reading "Risky Living", God began to reveal to me where the roots of my sins began and persisted. It began with unforgiveness. I had an unforgiving heart. I would eventually learn that it took root at the age of four, when I was molested by the neighborhood boys.

As I'd be reading along, God would put the face of someone who had hurt me in my mind. I would relive the event where I had chosen unforgiveness and allowed the root of bitterness to take up residence. It was frustrating, because I really wanted to read the book, but God kept interrupting me with these images from my past. I would be overcome by a deep conviction that I had to stop and deal with what He was showing me, or else I wouldn't be able to move forward, with the book or, more importantly, with my healing.

I learned early on, it's easier to just yield to God. After all, I had asked Him to help me. While I have a very strong will, His is stronger and He is persistent. I often describe this period of healing as, looking into the abyss of my heart – for as God shed His light on it, I realized how truly black it had become. A deep, dark pit. The word scars didn't accurately describe them – it was more like an ugly, oozing, pus-filled wound. Really, a sickening sight to behold.

So, when God showed me someone that I hadn't forgiven, I would kneel by my bedside and pray. In the beginning, He started with fresh hurts – folks that had recently offended me. Up until that point in my life, I was very, easily offended. I've heard some folks describe this process as "peeling an onion", though an actual onion smells far better than the ugliness that God was exposing in my soul. It was putrid.

Nevertheless, let me tell you, I got honest with God – telling Him all about the pain each person caused me and how they deserved my anger. Always, God would follow with an overwhelming conviction of my own sins I had committed against Him and others that I had disappointed in my past. Often the verse, *Matthew 7: 2 "For with what judgment ye judge, ye shall be judged: and with what measure ye mete, it shall be measured to you again"*, came up in my reading. *He made it clear to me, we* all will be judged the same way we judge others. And truly, was their sin against me, any worse than my sin against God or anyone else? In the end, I would choose to forgive that person and after a bit, I would feel the peace of God come over me.

I'd resume reading the book and before I knew it, here would come another face, and God and I would take yet another stroll into the abyss of my heart. This went on for several weeks. I told you, I was a mess! I had even confessed to Rose what God was doing in my heart and I know, the faithful, prayer warrior she is, she was praying for me all along.

The further back God took me, the more painful the memories, the more painful looking into the abyss became. Yet I knew that I had to do this – God had made progress already peeling back many layers, and I couldn't give up now. My heart felt like it was going to rip right out of my chest most nights. God truly was performing a surgery on me.

There's a scene in C.S. Lewis's story "Chronicles of Narnia - The Voyage of the Dawntreader", where Eustice had made the mistake of putting on the bracelet that turned him into the feared dragon (me) and try as he might, he couldn't tear off the dragon skin (my sin) to become a boy again (the woman God intended me to be).   So, Aslan, the Lion (God) had to do it for him...

"Then the lion said —You will have to let me undress you. I was afraid of his claws, I can tell you, but I was pretty, nearly desperate now. So, I just lay flat down on my back to let him do it.

"The very first tear he made was so deep that I thought it had gone right into my heart. And when he began pulling the skin off, it hurt worse than anything I've ever felt. The only thing that made me able to bear it was just the pleasure of feeling the stuff peel off. It hurts like billy-oh, but it is such fun to see it coming away."

"Well, he peeled the beastly stuff right off – and there it was lying on the grass, only ever so much thicker, and darker, and more knobbly-looking than the others had been. And there was I smooth and soft as a peeled switch and smaller than I had been. Then he caught hold of me – I didn't like that much for I was very tender underneath now that I'd no skin on — and threw me into the water. It smarted like anything but only for a moment. After that it became perfectly delicious and as soon as I started swimming and splashing, I found that all the pain had gone from my arm. And then I saw why. I'd turned into a boy again. . .."

This is exactly how I felt as God continued His work on me – peeling off the ugly "*knobbly-looking*" layers. But with each layer that was torn away, "*it smarted like anything but only for a moment*". I felt myself becoming far more than just human again. I was becoming the daughter of the King that He had intended me to be and it felt "perfectly delicious"!

13 GOING DOWN TO THE MAT

By this point, I had forgiven co-workers, friends, acquaintances, people in drive-through windows that had irritated me (yes, I was petty!), family members, old-neighbors, and school-mates. The list was so long. Seriously, I wondered if we would ever get to the end of it. Weeks had turned into months – I didn't see the end in sight!   However, now God was going to the darkest recesses of my heart.   The pain from my childhood – the origin of where I bought the lies of the enemy.

It was really, hard at first, and believe me, I resisted.   This area of my heart held the most familiar pain – the longest protected areas by the rage that yet, still simmered beneath the surface. First, He had me deal with forgiving the neighborhood boys that had abused me, at age four. While it was challenging, time and distance, and the fact that I really, didn't know them, helped me to let it go.

However, I remember when He first brought the face of the boy who had molested me, when I was between the age of eight to ten, to my mind, I was furious! NO WAY! Are you SERIOUS, God!?! You expect me, to forgive HIM!?! This person was closer – I still knew him. God's answer was simple: Yes. And He didn't back down.

I admit, this one almost derailed the whole process.   I was truly angry that God was expecting me to forgive this person who had done a considerable amount of damage to my psyche as a child. Yet God remained steadfast. I was so upset by the thought that I avoided my quiet time with Him for a couple of weeks. I just didn't want to deal with it, so I didn't. But I felt myself falling back into the dark despair that He had started bringing me out of. And He left me there - to simmer in my juices for a while. God won't make us do anything – our healing is our choice. He was there in the wings waiting for me to get over myself enough to let Him continue the work that He had begun.

Philippians 1:6 Being confident of this very thing, that he which hath begun a good work in you will perform it until the day of Jesus Christ

Finally, after a couple weeks of stewing, I decided I was going to prove to God why I shouldn't have to forgive this person who had hurt me so deeply. I decided God and I were going to go down to the mat, and one of us wasn't coming back up! Clearly, I thought way more of myself than I ever should have. So, that night, I closed my door (envision boxing gloves on both hands!) and sat down on my bedroom floor with my Bible, notebooks and Christian books surrounding me. I started digging through the scripture, looking for something in there to help my cause. But, I only found conviction, and confirmation that God's expectation for us to forgive, is the only way.

I ended up in Matthew 18 – the forgiveness chapter. I ran

across a verse that I hadn't remembered reading before, ***Matthew 18:18 Verily I say unto you, whatsoever ye shall bind on earth shall be bound in heaven; and whatsoever ye shall loose on earth shall be loosed in heaven***. God gave me revelation that when I hold unforgiveness in my heart towards someone, I interfere with the Holy Spirit's ability to convict the person of the sin they committed against me. What's bound on earth is bound in heaven! It says it clearly and the whole chapter is about forgiveness, so I know that's exactly what He was saying. Only through my forgiveness of this person, will the Holy Spirit begin to move in that person's life – to convict him of the sin he committed against me. This new truth he revealed was mind blowing! The thought, that God gives us the power to bind someone like that. But it was right there! In black and white!

The weight of that responsibility hit me like a brick. As angry and hurt as I was, I didn't wish harm on this person – I only wanted to continue justifying my anger towards him. It was my safe place. But I wondered if my unforgiveness was hindering him from knowing Christ.

The responsibility for that was too much. As I began praying, I felt the tears come. I started out, sitting cross-legged on the floor. By the end of my prayers, three hours later, I was prostrate, face-down on the floor. Both, the carpet and the pages of my Bible, were wet with my tears.

I knew I couldn't bind this person to damnation – I knew he wasn't a believer, and I felt overwhelming conviction that my unforgiveness might be getting in the way of him coming to know Christ. I had inflicted enough hurt on many people already. My heart was still ugly. But, being the cause of someone not finding their way to God, was not something I wanted. In the end, not only did I choose to forgive him, but I surrendered my heart and life to God that night. I promised God that I would not resist His work in me.

Remember how I said when the night started, that one of us wasn't coming up? Praise God, it was true. One of us didn't come up! The ugly old me was left on that floor and God raised up the new me! I finally, fully understood the verse in *2 Corinthians 5:17 Therefore if any man be in Christ, he is a new creature: old things are passed away; behold, all things are become new.*

14 WHAT IS LOOSED ON EARTH
IS LOOSED IN HEAVEN

Deuteronomy 30: 6 And the LORD thy God will circumcise thine heart, and the heart of thy seed, to love the LORD thy God with all thine heart, and with all thy soul,

that thou mayest live.

As I sat up after praying that night, I felt the Holy Spirit telling me to write him a letter. Again, mind blown! But I figured God knew what He was doing, and I was on such a high from the weight of that unforgiveness being lifted - so I complied. I wrote page after page, but instead of writing to the man he had become, I wrote it to the boy who had committed the sin against me, venting all the frustration and pain I had felt from the abuse. I then concluded the letter, that I forgave him and prayed for God to do a work in his heart and bring him healing. When I was done, I sat there looking at it, wondering if God was going to tell me to mail it to him. Thankfully - He didn't. Instead I put it in a sealed envelope and put it in the cover of my Bible, where it remains to this day.

God worked a miracle in my heart that night, but my loosing this man of the unforgiveness, also loosed the Spirit's ability to move in his life – and God was about to reveal yet another miracle from this act of obedience! About a month later, I got a phone call that this man had received Christ as his Savior! Mind blown again! The power of God and the truth of His Word can't be denied!

It was not a coincidence that God revealed this truth to me and then from my obedience, he was released from the bonds that I had held against him for 23 years and now, he had given his heart to Christ!!! Now, could God have saved Him without my forgiveness? Yes, God is way bigger than me and my will. His desire is for all to come to know Him. Had I not discovered and exercised this truth, He likely would have gotten to the man another way, but I would still be mired in the ugliness of my past. I believe He allowed this to play out this way to show me, just how powerful forgiveness and adhering to His Word truly is!

While He had done a tremendous work in my heart, I still had a long way to go. I can't lie and say it got easier – giving up old pain and familiar spirits was difficult. Even though I had surrendered the pain, I would sometimes find myself missing my old companion, rage. I'd entertain thoughts that would try to pull me right back down into the pit. There were still many deep hurts and old sins that I had yet to deal with too. But I was determined to allow God to remove the masks that had covered my life. And I had a new revelation of the power that dwelt within me and I was learning how to operate in the Holy Spirit daily.

Ezekiel 36:26 I will give you a new heart and put a new spirit in you. I will remove your heart of stone and give you a heart of flesh.

15 GOD FORGIVES THE WORST SINS

God had shaken up my world. Before I had time to adjust to this new sense of being, He was leading me down into the abyss again. With all that He had delivered me from to this point, it's probably shocking that I still refer to my heart as the "abyss". But it was and if I'm not mindful of my spiritual walk, I believe it could be again. However, this time, He wasn't dealing with other's sins against me, but my own sins, past and present.

He began with relationships, where I had sinned against others. The conviction fell on me hard and I wept each time God brought the image of someone I had cared about into my mind, that I had mistreated. My parents, siblings, my kids, and friends; again, the list was long. As He walked me through this process, I would confess the sin, repent and I'd try to make restitution with the person.

He also taught me a new principal – receiving His forgiveness. I'm not sure if you've experienced this – though I'd lay odds you have – but you pray your prayer of repentance and ask for forgiveness. Then go on your merry way, only to fall into the very same conviction again – same sin – and back on our knees begging for the same forgiveness, all over again! Why, oh why do we do that!?! I believe it's because we don't make that mental choice to RECEIVE His forgiveness.

Just as forgiving someone is a choice, so is receiving forgiveness, also a choice. The Lord began to bring His verse **Psalm 103:12 *As far as the east is from the west, so far has he removed our transgressions from us***, into my brain again. Each time I'd try to drag up that old guilt and shame for a sin already confessed and forgiven, God would remind me – often I could hear Him say, "What sin!?!". Here it is folks, when God forgives, He REWRITES our history! That's an awesome concept to ponder – seriously! Think about it! When I confessed my sins and asked for forgiveness, He was faithful to forgive my sins. He wiped my slate clean. It is as though I never committed those sins! Now THAT, is praise worthy – not of me, but of the Almighty God! Happy dance!

Thank God He revealed this to me, because now He was about to lead me into the deepest part of the blackness in my heart - I was a murderer. I don't say that to hurt anyone else who has walked that path, but this is how I felt about myself. Three times, I was responsible for ending the life of a child – my children! I don't know that I can ever convey the weight I felt when the conviction of God came falling on me that night. Those three little creatures that God had put in me had a purpose – a life – that I ended. It was overwhelming! I was a heap on the floor again – sobbing my heart out – fully broken for the sin and blackness of my heart. How could God ever forgive me for destroying those three little lives!?! The struggle didn't end that night – it carried on for weeks!

As hard as I fought to not forgive others who had sinned deeply against me, I found myself fighting even harder, to not receive God's forgiveness for my own sin.   I felt so unworthy – I am still so unworthy – of God's forgiveness.   Yet He held it out to me, on a gold platter.   All I had to do was reach out and take it.

Galatians 2:21 I do not set aside the grace of God, for if righteousness could be gained through the law, Christ died for nothing!

I encountered the verse Galatians 2:21 and one night, it hit me.   How could I NOT receive this gift that God wants to freely, and lovingly, give me!?!   To deny the gift of forgiveness, means that Christ died in vain!   It would mean that He suffered and bled for nothing!   Again, the convicting power of the Holy Spirit fell on me like a great weight.   My unwillingness to accept forgiveness, was in, itself a sin against God – against His Son who died for me!   So, then I was back on my face begging for forgiveness for yet another sin against the Almighty and His beloved son.

I conceded.   I gave up the fight.   I made the choice to receive His forgiveness for taking the lives of three innocents.   I remember laying across my bed, tears streaming down my face, as I imagined the Father's arms wrapped around me – comforting me – though I didn't deserve it.   And the weight of those sins, was gone.

Don't get me wrong – the memory and the conviction of what I did is still there. I will always understand that fact. They will never leave me entirely – I don't want them to. I want to remember so that I never fall into that pit again! But Christ bore the weight of those sins on the cross. They're no longer mine to carry. Never would I want Him to think I'm not grateful for what He did for me.

So, I humbly received His forgiveness. I walk in that forgiveness. I CHOOSE daily - sometimes minute by minute - to make forgiveness a habit I exercise. My feelings don't always want to comply, but I've learned that my will is strong. I CHOOSE to forgive with my WILL and guess what!?! My feelings eventually catch up! Helping others understand this most, POWERFUL concept of forgiveness, became part of my new purpose in life. Most struggles in life can be tied back to the root of unforgiveness, somewhere in our past.

16 NEW MINISTRY

After a couple years of continually immersing myself in His Word, (around Easter, 2001) I had another powerful experience with God. I had run across a writing on the internet, which described the crucifixion process. I had never known the full details of what they did to Jesus, only the sanitized version, so that document was extremely enlightening and troubling. It was graphic and left me sleepless for several nights. The Holy Spirit was still doing a deep work in my heart and I found myself at the alter the following Sunday, Easter morning.

Before, I had surrendered myself to His service and to His will for my healing. This new breaking that He was walking me through that morning in the service was different. For the first time, I truly – deeper than I thought possible - empathized with the pain and suffering that Jesus Christ allowed himself to be subjected to - because of me. For the first time, I had truly personalized what salvation really, meant and to what extreme God went to - not only for me, but for all of us.

With this revelation, I felt the Holy Spirit speak to my heart. He told me I would be teaching soon. This new understanding that I had, for the depth of God's love and forgiveness, was another message He expected me to share. I was terrified and excited at the same time. I had no idea who, what, when or where I would be teaching, but I knew I had to wait for God to tell me - and He did.

I had been mentoring a couple of women at my job. One day, shortly after Easter, out of the blue, one of the ladies asked me if I would lead a Bible study, right there at Evenflo. I had immediate peace in my spirit that this was God's will – He had already given me the "What" to teach, now He provided the "Who" and the "Where". All that remained was the "When". This same woman made contact with other Christians in our office and before I knew it, we had about 20 different folks (a mix of male and female), wanting to come. One of them was a Vice President of Sales. He suggested booking a large conference room, over a lunch period, one day a week. So, I did, and the Bible study began.

I was really, green in the beginning – so unsure of myself. I had taught individuals, but this was my first-time teaching in a group setting. I fumbled my way thru the first few lessons and was ready to give up, not sure that anyone was getting anything out of it. But God sent people in the group (including the VP) to encourage me to not give up. Over time and with practice, I felt God strengthening me and giving me the Words and the voice to teach His Word.

Earlier, I had mentioned how the devil used one of my weaknesses to stifle my work for God. And he tried again. Part of the struggle was that I talk soft and sometimes fast – to the point of stumbling over my words. But I cried out to God – He put me in this position – He had to be the one to help me through this.

Also, as I mentioned earlier, when you cry out to God, He always answers. This time, He did with this verse, ***Psalm 81:10 I am the Lord your God, who brought you out of the land of Egypt; <u>open your mouth WIDE, and I will fill it</u>.*** I love this verse! Not only did He give it to me back then, but He recently reminded me of this again, while writing my story! I surrendered my life to His service. He had told me I would teach and proclaim His glory to others. Therefore, He will tell me what to say and when to say it. All I need to do is open my mouth WIDE and He will fill it! This created a boldness in me and stripped away the fear that wanted to derail me from ministry.

Now, don't get me wrong, I still get butterflies when I speak in front of a group of people, or even as I'm driving to meet someone for counseling. I find myself with sweaty palms and mind racing, wondering if they're going to ask me something that I won't be able to answer. But I've learned each time, to submit myself fully to the Lord and to hold on to that promise that "if I open my mouth, He will fill it". It's not up to me to do the work – God promises that if I obey, He'll give me what I need.

Each time I'm in one of those situations, I pray that God removes me from the equation and allows me only to be a conduit of His spirit, flowing through me, to the person or persons, to whom I'm ministering. Every time, He is faithful. It excites my heart when I make eye contact with someone and I see they've had a revelation. All I am is the vessel - the revelation comes from the Holy Spirit. Praise God!

I felt His presence moving within the group. There was a lot of upheaval at Evenflo. There had been a lot of lay-offs, and over time, several in the group were no longer with the company. Yet, during that time, all of us had complete peace that God was at work in each of our lives, regardless of what was happening within the company. If it was our time to leave, then we fully believed that God had something better for us.

The Bible study carried on over the next 3 years. Over time, I had people coming from all different types of religions; Catholic, Mormon, Jehovah's Witness, Buddhism, and every mainstream denomination. I determined to teach God's truth and not allow the "religious traditions" or "false doctrine" to have any leeway in the meetings. The reality is that I have no idea if anything I taught during that time impacted those that came from false religions. But I'm confident that God knows, and seeds of His truth will always produce fruit. *Isaiah 55:11 It is the same with my word. I send it out, and it always produces fruit. It will accomplish all that I want it to, and it will prosper everywhere I send it.* I had to trust then and still do now, that when He gives me a Word to speak, it's up to Him to touch hearts – my only job is to deliver the message.

It was during this time that God also used me to guide a friend through healing from marital infidelity. She was seeking to grow deeper when the enemy set out to derail her. She found out that her husband had been having an affair. She asked me one day, what she should do – whether to divorce him or not. I think because I was divorced, she was expecting me to say, "go ahead - divorce him", but I couldn't. Since my rededication to Christ, God had convicted me about how important marriage is to Him. All I could tell her is what the Word of God says. I asked her if she wanted to know what God thought about it. She responded that she did. So, I walked her through the scripture. I told her that the scripture tells us restoration should be sought if, at all possible. Her husband had humbled himself and sought her forgiveness, so it was possible, from his perspective. Now all she needed to do was align her perspective with God's.

I counseled her that God considers marriage sacred and a lifelong union. Jesus spoke in *Matthew 19:6*, that man and woman are no longer two but one flesh and what God has joined, no man should separate. God hates divorce *(Malachi 2:13-16)* and only allowed Moses to institute it because of the hardness of man's heart *(Matthew 19:8)*, but it was never what God had intended. Both Testaments teach that the only grounds for divorce is adultery. So clearly, she had Biblical grounds. However, her husband confessed and repented and was seeking restoration. While divorce may have been morally ok for her, it was not required by God. Better yet, it was not DESIRED by God. The responsibility of that decision lay solely upon her shoulders.

After many hours of counseling, it became evident to me that she didn't want the marriage to end. So, I began to focus on teaching her about forgiveness – even sharing parts of my story with her, about how I released the man who had abused me from unforgiveness and a month later He came to know Christ. It was a long process, many months of prayer and counseling and seeking scripture together. But thank God, she chose to take the road of forgiveness and last I heard, their marriage is still going strong.

Along with leading the Bible study at work, I was also working in the music ministry at Bethel. Eventually, I felt God call me to start a women's prayer group at the church. So, I did that as well. I asked four other women in the church to become a leader over a small group. We split up the names of the women in the church, so each of us had up to ten women in our group (it was a small church). The splitting up of the names was random to us, but not to God. It was mind blowing how He organized who ministered to whom.

The ladies that came to my group were, like me, divorcees or in troubled marriages. And a couple of them came out of "false doctrine" backgrounds. God had already prepared me for dealing with that through the Evenflo Bible study. Each group met once a week and our focus, was supposed to be prayer. However, my group became a counseling/prayer group as several were seeking healing themselves from either a current troubled marriage or a past divorce. I continually took them back to the Bible. Everything I advised was based on God's Word, not mine.

It was an amazing experience, getting to bond with those women. I love them dearly and pray for them as God brings them across my mind! It was exciting to see that God truly was using me and my past failures, to help others. I can tell you that each of those women today are walking strong in their faith. Not that it was me, but God working through me – being His mouth piece to speak truth into their lives – no compromise, even at risk of someone taking offense and leaving the group. But no one did – God's grace flourished in that group of women.

One of my dearest friends I had come to know through Bethel, was Lucille Martin, whom I affectionately call Mama Lu. She was older than me – old enough to be my mom, and we clicked right from the start. When we first met, she was a brand-new Christian. We quickly grew close, and I mentored her in the Word.

Lucy had a hunger for God's Word and she was faithful to study. She soon learned the power of prayer and felt called to be an Intercessor. I know that she spent hours in the Word and prayer daily. It was her passion – she loved her time with God. I also know she kept me, and my kids covered in prayer. I referred to both her and Rose as my personal "Prayer Warriors". At any time, I know I could call them or email them with a problem and they'd immediately go to war on my behalf. I could feel their prayers! I believe they both are the sort of woman that when they go down on their knees in prayer - demons shudder.

God continued to surround me with many amazing Christian women. One such woman, Vareena, became a very good friend to me, for many years. When I first met her, she had just come out of The World Church in South Africa. She knew all about God and Jesus, but the Holy Spirit was a completely foreign concept to her. While she believed that Jesus had existed, she had never given her heart to Him. Her husband, had recently been saved. So, she had him on one side of her, praying for her and teaching her. Then she had me on the other side, praying for her and talking to her about the Holy Spirit. Her house keeper was also born again and talking to her about knowing Christ. Later, we laughed about how she didn't have a chance to not come to accept Jesus, with it coming at her from all sides.

After months of both her husband and I faithfully committing her to Christ in prayer, she had an encounter with Jesus and His Holy Spirit one morning, while walking on the treadmill. By the time He was done dealing with her, she had surrendered her heart to Jesus and became a powerhouse in ministry for Christ. Both Vareena, and her husband, played a significant role in my final healing years later.

Over the following years, God continued to work in and through me. I was learning how to live by faith, not my feelings. Key word was "learning", it took me many years to mature in this area. Though being human, I know if I let my guard down, I can easily slip back into old habits. God, in His grace and mercy, had looked beyond the filth in my heart and while His forgiveness removed the stain, He still, continued to do the work to remove the pain, one piece at a time. I mentioned one verse that He continually brought to my mind when I would try to "re-own" something He had already forgiven me for. ***Psalm 103:12 As far as the east is from the west, so far hath he removed our transgressions from us.***

Even though God had done a tremendous work in my life, I was still struggling with depression and sad to admit - feelings of self-hatred. Remember, I said it took years and lots of pain for God to work ALL those strongholds out of me. However, the more I sought God, the more grounded in His truth I became. But try as I might, I couldn't put my finger on it, there was still something beneath the surface - festering. I believed in my heart that some way, somehow, He would fully heal me. Yet there was still work in my heart to be done.

17 SINGLE – TO BE OR NOT TO BE

Several years after the divorce, God revealed it was time to deal with forgiving the "ex". At that point, I hadn't seen him or heard from him for almost a decade. Also, I had never received the first child support payment from him. He was on the lam – running from paying child support. The court systems had not been able to catch up with him. My understanding was that he was job jumping or getting paid under the table. All in order to not fulfill his responsibility to his kids. Yet God wanted me to forgive the bum! Yep – he was a bum! This was another tough one to deal with – I didn't want to forgive him. Yet I knew that not too, would stifle my growth. God had already convicted me, now it was just a matter of aligning my will to God's.

I mentioned earlier that I was reading a book "Shattering Your Strongholds" by Liberty Savard. One of the principals she focused on (referencing Matthew 18) was the "binding" of our will to the will of God. Remember, what's bound on earth is bound in heaven and vice versa. So, the same principal that God revealed to me about forgiveness, she applied to binding our soul (i.e. our mind, will and emotions) to God. It was a new concept to me, but it made sense.

I was struggling with forgiving Ed, and I knew that God wanted me to be free, so every day, I began to pray that verse over my own soul. Binding my will to God's will. Binding my mind to the mind of Christ. Binding my heart/emotions to the heart of God. Again, God did a miraculous work in my heart. One day as I was driving home, I was praying this verse over my will, my heart and my mind and was overcome with a sense of relief. I felt the release. I released Ed from ALL the hurt and the hatefulness that he had done to me. At the same time, I felt the Holy Spirit speak to my spirit and I knew I was completely released from that marriage.

Before this point, I knew I couldn't remarry – I had too much resentment and frustration with the failed marriage. Had I walked into another relationship, that baggage would have been carried right in and probably would have destroyed any new relationship as well. But now I was free! It was like a breath of fresh air! I knew that if I now chose to remarry, it was ok, both with God and, with me. There had been opportunities – men who had pursued me. But I put them off in the past because I knew I was too broken, and I didn't want to ruin more lives. But now, hmm, where do I go!?!

Even though I had chosen to remain single, I struggled with loneliness and often wished I had a husband. I just wanted to feel "normal". I knew that God was also working in me to be free from that "need". He was working in me to fully, seek Him to fulfill what I thought I needed. This was a new area of surrender that He was walking me through. He gave me the verses in ***Psalm 40:1-3 I waited patiently for the Lord; and he inclined unto me*** *and heard my cry. He brought me up also out of a horrible pit, out of the miry clay, and set my feet upon a rock, and established my goings. And he hath put a new song in my mouth, even praise unto our God: many shall see it, and fear, and shall trust in the Lord*. I know God was telling me that this was my future – that He was nowhere near done using me to reach others. But at this point He wanted my full focus. He had brought me so far up out of that "miry clay".

Miry clay is defined as "swampy, muddy" or "one who cannot find a foothold but slips and sinks". I occasionally still found myself falling back into dark thinking, but God was always right there – hand stretched out to pull me back up out of the thick of the mire. How could I not praise Him and allow Him to continue His work in my life!?! He revealed to me that a lot of my discontent was unmet expectations. My imagined "need" to be "normal" and to "fit in" with my married friends. At that point, most of my friends were married, not singles.

So, I surrendered my desire to marry. This is a tricky one, because I've had to surrender this one multiple times (laugh with me here, folks!). My heart wanted to be in line with God's will, but many times, I'd catch myself knocking God off the throne and climbing up on His seat – you know, trying to be Lord of my life again. Then the conviction would come, I'd beg for forgiveness, and scamper down off His throne, and allow Christ to take His seat again. Quite funny to imagine that scene. Imagine, big throne, big God, little me, trying to scramble up and down the leg of his throne, while God stands there, kicked back, arms crossed, patiently waiting for me to get off His throne!!

Then one day, God gave me revelation. Not once did He say, I would NEVER have a chance at marriage again. Just not now! His goal was to get me into a place where I live in the moment – not the past or the future - and where my true needs were met solely by Him. There isn't a man alive that can meet all my needs, so why try to put that responsibility on any man. Only God can fulfill all my needs.

He continued to show me that what I perceived as a "need" for intimacy or to feel normal, is a desire, not a need. God too promises He will fulfill the desires of my heart – His Word says that clearly in *Psalm 37:4b He will give you the desire of your heart*. Whoa! Wait! Let's back this bus up! Let's read the WHOLE verse: *Psalm 37:4 <u>Delight yourself in the LORD</u> and THEN <u>He will give you the desire of your heart</u>*. The truth of this scripture says that we only get the desire of our heart, AFTER, we delight ourselves in the Lord. I've heard so many people quote this and completely misconstrue the message God is trying to teach. Usually, they leave off that first part altogether, or falsely, teach that "delight" means to just be happy in service of God. Well, I mean, golly gee-whiz – I've been "happy" in the work of the Lord, yet He wasn't fulfilling this "desire" of mine! All that brought was condemnation and self-doubt about my service! I knew God wasn't in that line of thinking.

Here's what I believe it really, means.   To delight in something means that you find your greatest joy, in whatever, is the object of your affection.   God wants to be that object of our affection.   He wants to be our greatest Joy! As we grow closer to Him, He changes the desire of our heart and then we really, begin to delight ourselves in Him, and THEN we get the desires of our heart!   God's desires become our desires!

We do that by talking to Him, reading His Word and walking out our faith in His service.   We also do that by making God our go-to person.   When good things happen, go to God and thank Him.   When bad things happen, go to God and still thank Him.   When nothing is happening, go to God and thank Him that no calamity has come your way and ask for His continued guidance! Thankfulness is the key – God loves a thankful heart.

Ultimately what He's trying to teach us is what the Bible calls, "praying without ceasing". It doesn't mean non-stop prayer -it's just a regularly reoccurring discussion with God, like you'd have with your best friend.   Think about it – if your best friend is standing beside you, you're likely to have a conversation – right!?! That's all God is asking of us – to talk to Him.   *1 Thessalonians 5:16-18*   *16Rejoice always, 17pray continually, 18give thanks in all circumstances; for this is God's will for you in Christ Jesus.* If you have any question about God's will for your life – start with that verse – it's pretty, clear – He wants a close relationship with you. That's His will for your life!

18 MY WICKED TONGUE

I mentioned earlier, God had also taught me the power of praying scripture. One that I prayed regularly – and still do – is *Psalm 139:23-24 Search me, God, and know my heart; test me and know my anxious thoughts. See if there is any offensive way in me and lead me in the way everlasting*. God knows, there's still plenty of offensive ways in me and it's a continual process to this day, weeding those out. One thing I'm certain of, is that when we pray scripture, God sits up and takes notice.   His Word is perfect and it's divine.   Seriously, how could He not pay attention to and respond to His own Word!?!

Another group of verses I came to rely on was *Ephesians 6:16-18 In addition to all this, take up the shield of faith, with which you can extinguish all the flaming arrows of the evil one. Take the helmet of salvation and the sword of the Spirit, which is the word of God. And pray in the Spirit on all occasions with all kinds of prayers and requests. With this in mind, be alert and always keep on praying for all the Lord's people*. He was teaching me to discard the old armor I wore; pride, haughtiness and the rage that would come out by way of my tongue (my words), and to put on His armor; faith, salvation and His Word on my tongue! While He had brought me far, these old habits liked to rear their head from time to time.   But God is faithful and when I'm faithful in return, He grows me a bit more in my spiritual walk or as the scripture puts it *2 Corinthians 3:18 But we all, with* *unveiled face, beholding as in a mirror the glory of the Lord, are being transformed into the same image from <u>glory to glory</u>, just as from the Lord, the Spirit.*

When He began to deal with me about my tongue, it again was quite painful. This time, it involved an incident where I felt I needed to defend my son. While God had done a significant work in my heart and the rage I had felt for so long, had mostly dissipated, I still had a major issue with my tongue. Especially when I got upset or angered about anything.

I was still quite gifted at giving a good tongue lashing. The difference now, was the Holy Spirit would convict me and I'd have to go back and apologize for it. Before God changed my heart, there wasn't a chance I would apologize. And, also, I no longer enjoyed destroying people with my tongue. God had healed those places and I no longer felt the need to share my pain.

You would think it would be easier to bite my tongue, than to have to go back and apologize, but it always seemed to get the best of me. I knew what God's Word had to say about the tongue in *James 3:4-6 Consider ships as well. Although they are so large and are driven by strong winds, they are steered by a very small rudder wherever the pilot is inclined. In the same way, the tongue is a small part of the body, but it boasts of great things. Consider how small a spark sets a great forest ablaze. The tongue also is a fire, a world of wickedness among the parts of the body.*

It pollutes the whole person, sets the course of his life on fire, and is itself set on fire by hell.

One night as I was studying, it occurred to me, why not ask God to bind my tongue to His will (back to Matthew 18). It worked for forgiveness and for changing my heart, mind and emotions, why wouldn't it work for helping me to control my tongue. So, I began to pray that God would bind my tongue to His will. It wasn't long before it was tested.

My son had been bullied at school for quite a while. One day, he had reached his limit and struck back at a couple of the kids who were tormenting him. The leader of the gang was a very troubled girl whose family had a lot of influence with the school board. As a result of my son's conflict with the girl, the school's Assistant principal called me and gave ME a tongue lashing. He assumed that just because Aaron came from a "broken" home that his outburst was due to a poor home environment. He knew the girl's family and of course, she had done no wrong – the fault was entirely my son's!

Now before, I would have probably hung up the phone, driven to the school, met him face to face, and ripped that principal a new one (Christian school or not). I used to enjoy watching a man – or whoever happened to be the object of my rage - become completely demoralized, by what came out of my mouth. And I can tell you, it would have been peppered with plenty of expletives! I wouldn't have stopped until I had reduced the man to a crumbling heap on the floor. I was gifted (or cursed!), however you want to look at it.

However, God had begun a new work in me. He answered my prayers and this time, you know what He did!?! He literally tongue-tied me! Seriously! Tongue - tied! My tongue would NOT move! I couldn't utter anything beyond a gasp. I just stood there, listening to this "Christian" man berate me – making unfounded accusations against me. Simply because I was a divorcee.

He finished his discourse against me and all I could do was just hang up the phone. This time, it was me that crumbled to the floor. Why would God allow this man to talk to me like that? I am divorced, but I didn't leave the marriage – we were abandoned. This man knew nothing of the solid, safe, secure, home I had built for my kids. He knew nothing of the Christ-centered principals that I taught my kids daily. Yet he arrogantly accused and belittled me. Hmmm – kind of sounds like something I had done in the past! *Destroy, and don't worry about asking questions later.* That was my motto. God had allowed me to get a taste of my own medicine.

That night, I sought the Word – I begged God to give me some sign that He was working. He had bound my tongue and kept me from defending myself and my son. I kept saying, "What are you doing God?!". I was falling into that victim mentality again. But He responded, "Just what you asked me to do". In my quiet time that night, He led me to several scriptures.

>*Exodus 14:14 The LORD will fight for you;*
>*you need only to be still."*

>*2 Chronicles 20:17 You will not have to fight this battle. Take up*
>*your positions; stand firm and see the deliverance*
>*the LORD will give you, Judah and Jerusalem.*
>*Do not be afraid; do not be discouraged.*
>*Go out to face them tomorrow, and the LORD will be with you.'"*

>*Deuteronomy 1:30 The LORD your God, who is going before*
>*you, will fight for you, as he did for you in Egypt,*
>*before your very eyes,*

>*Deuteronomy 20:4 For the LORD your God is the one who goes*
>*with you to fight for you against your enemies*
>*to give you victory."*

There it was, in black and white. All those years, I would fight anyone and everyone, to defend myself and my own. Not only fight, but I'd tear them to shreds. Now, I was on the receiving end and I couldn't even open my mouth to defend myself. But here, God was showing me that if I would just "**be** still" – "**stand firm and see**" - just "**remain - in Him**". Then He would fight **this** battle – not MY battle, **THIS** battle - for me. The battles were no longer mine to fight – they all belong to God! I meditated on those verses that He gave me and decided I would drive Aaron to school the next day and talk with the Head principal.

As I pulled up and parked in front of the school the next morning, we noticed a couple of police cars parked in front of Dayton Christian school. Aaron said, "Mama look!". The doors opened, and the police escorted the girl – the very same one that had been tormenting my son – out of the school - in hand cuffs! We watched as they put her in the back of the police car and drove off. Both the head principal and the assistant were standing there by the door, looking stunned.

As Aaron and I walked up, the assistant principal had a sheepish look on his face – like maybe, he was feeling a bit convicted about the way he treated me on the phone. Regardless, the truth I believe had been revealed and praise God, I didn't have to say a word! God had gone before me – fought the battle - before my very eyes! It was over, and thankfully, I didn't have to apologize to anyone! Ha!

It always takes surrender – continued surrender. It's not a one-time thing and done. We will fight against our cursed, human nature, as well as the spiritual principalities that rule this earth until the day God takes us home.

Ephesians 6:12 For our struggle is not against flesh and blood, but against the rulers, against the powers, against the world forces of this darkness, against the spiritual forces of wickedness in the heavenly places.

This is the process of sanctification and it won't end until we see glory. I've found that, if I stay in His Word and in communication with the Almighty, the battles that are waged against me, and within me, are shorter lived and easier to overcome. The sword that I now wield in battle is God's Word of truth, instead of the raging tongue of self-centeredness, unforgiveness and un-surrendered pain.

I'm continually amazed at Christians I encounter who have the greatest weapon of all ages, within their grasp, but instead of taking it up and using it the way God intended, they languish in pain and suffering, and question why (!?!). And this is not the kind of pain and suffering that brings glory to God - so it's all in vain. Let that sink in. If God doesn't get the glory for it, it's all - for - nothing! If they'd only surrender and submit to God's way. If they'd only pick up the Word of God and ingest it daily, how peaceful their life would become. Here I am, chuckling at myself. Just look at how long it took me to learn that very same lesson!

To further my healing, He taught me to personalize His Word. My favorite is still ***Eph 3:16-21 I pray that out of his glorious*** *riches he may strengthen you (ME) with power through his Spirit in your (MY) inner being, [17] so that Christ may dwell in your (MY) hearts through faith. And I pray that you (I), being rooted and established in love, [18] may have power, together with all the Lord's holy people, to grasp how wide and long and high and deep is the love of Christ, [19] and to know this love that surpasses knowledge—that you (I) may be filled to the measure of all the fullness of God. [20] Now to him who is able to do immeasurably more than all we (I) ask or imagine, according to his power that is at work within us (ME), [21] to him be glory in the church and in Christ Jesus throughout all generations, for ever and ever! Amen.*

His promise is that as I seek Him, He will strengthen me, dwell in me, keep me rooted in Him and love me, unlike I've ever experienced love before. He still wants to do a powerful work through my life – much of which I may never see the end-result and may only learn about when I get to heaven. The work that I do now, for Christ, will affect my future generations – my kids, my grandkids and their kids! My family heritage of faith will live on!

19 FREE AT LAST!

You would think by now, I should be riding high, right!?! Me too. Yet, there was still something, hidden deep in me that I still could not put my finger on. Occasionally, I'd find myself slipping into dark thoughts and depression again. I kept praying and asking God, "Ok Lord, what's the deal!?!". I'd search scripture and go back through memories. I'd forgive all those from my past and ask forgiveness again for my sins, (you know, just in case one didn't take!?!), even though I knew they were covered. Yet, it persisted.

So here I was, this Christian teacher, a woman of God, that the Lord had brought up out of the mire, still struggling with depression and self-doubt about something hidden from me, that I couldn't get beyond. I was again struggling with insomnia and I was having massive migraines. My dentist said I had TMJ from grinding my teeth and clenching my jaws. It had gotten so bad, that I practically had lock-jaw. At one point, I hadn't been able to eat solid food for a couple of weeks. I could only drink liquids or anything I could take through a straw – though that was extremely painful too.

My friend, Vareena, and her husband, had invited me to join them in Cincinnati for a Call to All meeting. I have it noted in my journal as March 10, 2010. It was a gathering of multiple denominations, including Messianic Jews, to come together and

Praise God. We had worship services and then would break off and go into class rooms to listen to different speakers, on all types of Christ-centered teaching. While there, the intent was for me to meet their friend, Ford Taylor, and for him to pray over me. He was a tall, Texan, with a deep southern drawl. When I first met him, I was taken with the humility of his spirit and his gentleness, for such a big man – and a successful man at that. He had owned a very successful and lucrative company, that he gave up to serve God full-time.

Later in the morning, Ford, Steve, Vareena and I met up in the sanctuary, which was empty by that point. Ford started out asking me "What's your struggle?". So, I gave him a synopsis of my past (excluding my deepest, darkest sins, of course). I told him about all the abuse, my mother's generational curses, the eating disorders, the loss of my dad, the divorce, and that there was still something that I couldn't put my finger on that was dragging me down into depression, even though God had done so much work in my heart. I had insomnia and now TMJ – I can't eat – I can't sleep - I'm miserable! And yet, God is still working through me! What gives!?!

Well, it quickly became clear to me that this man had true discernment. He saw right through me. I know it wasn't him – it was the Holy Spirit in him, giving him the revelation. After I got through my diatribe, he sat quietly for a moment and then looked me square in the eye and in his deep, southern drawl, said "You haven't forgiven yourself". Jaw dropped - mind blown!

While Vareena and Steve had no knowledge of my deepest, darkest secrets, I truly believe that God revealed something of them, to Ford that day. He nailed it. As soon as the words came out of his mouth, I knew that was the "hidden" sin. I had not forgiven myself. I was forgiven by God – I had battled that and received His forgiveness, but not once did I consider that I had to forgive myself for anything. Vareena thought he meant that I hadn't forgiven myself for "allowing" (probably not the right word), myself to be abused, maybe?!

I knew exactly what he was talking about. I believe Ford knew – or at least had an inkling. Most certainly, God knew, that it was something much deeper, and darker. And…he continued, "You haven't forgiven God either". IF I could have opened my mouth, I believe my jaw would have hit the floor at this point.

He stood up and walked up to where I was sitting. Steve and Vareena sat on each side of me and grasped my hands. He apologized that he didn't have any oil to anoint me, so he licked his thumb and rubbed it on my forehead! Yes, I had a spit-shine anointing that day and we all had a good chuckle. He walked behind me and raised both hands above my head. At first, he was quiet – didn't say a word. Then he began to pray.

He started out by asking God to forgive him for falling into lust again a few days before – something about some cheerleaders.

Wait, say what!?! Then he asked God to forgive him for being short with his wife the day before. Um ok, this is weird!?! Then he explained, he didn't want any sin or unrighteousness in him, to hamper his prayer over me. WOW (emphasis added), new revelation! Then he began to pray for me.

One of the first things he said was, "on behalf of every man that ever hurt you, lied to you, betrayed you, abandoned you, or abused you - in any way, shape or form - I apologize to you on their behalf". Well, I crumbled. The tears flowed. Never had anyone in my life, ever - and I mean ever! - apologized to me for anything. Seriously! I distinctly remember I didn't sob or cry out loud, but the tears flowed – like they do today when the Holy Spirit falls on me. I couldn't utter a sound. I sat there, stunned, yet relieved. God had uncovered the sins that were wearing me down. And this man, humbled himself, on behalf of the male species and apologized - to me!

Then Ford asked me, "Are you willing to forgive yourself, for anything and everything of your past, that is holding you back?". I nodded yes – but he insisted I speak. So, I squeaked out, "yes". Then he asked me, "Are you willing to forgive God for allowing the atrocities that were committed against you to happen?". I nodded and squeaked out, "yes".

I can't tell you what he said after that point – all I know was that I was truly in the Spirit at that moment. Everything became surreal. My face was soaked with tears; I could feel them dropping on my hands, and Verena's and Steve's for that matter. I could sense Ford slightly moving his hands from the top of my head (never once touching my head), down the sides of my head, and as he did so, the heat in my head (from the TMJ which felt like it was on fire) and the pain that I was experiencing from the migraines and TMJ, began to ease and cool. By the time his hands rested on my shoulders, the migraine was gone, the TMJ pain was gone and the heat I felt in my entire head - was gone! Let me be clear, it was not Ford that accomplished this work – it was the one and only, true living God, that accomplished the healing. It was through Ford's obedience, to humbly, surrender himself to God's work, and through my obedience in choosing to forgive myself, and God!

I was finally free! Praise God, I AM FREE! When we finished praying and crying and hugging, we walked down to the cafeteria and the four of us sat down, and for the first time in weeks, I ate a sandwich. I couldn't believe it, yet it was real! I was healed - inside out. Vareena whooped with excitement when she saw I could chew my food. I was whooping with excitement, that God had lifted the depression off me and for the first time, in four, long decades – forty years, folks! Now, I am free! Though I sometimes fall into "ho-hum moods", I have not, since that day, fallen into a state of depression. Praise be to God alone!

Ps 143:8 In you I do trust, cause me to know the way in which I should walk, for I lift up my soul to You.

20 SURRENDER THE WHY'S

Throughout my whole life, there had been one question that I had continually asked God – well, during the periods of time that I was actually talking to Him anyway.   That question was, "Why?".   Why God, did you allow me to be molested by multiple people - multiple times?   Why, God did you take my daddy away in a time, when I needed him most?   Why did you let me meet Eddie?   Why God, did you allow me to kill my three babies?   Why?   Why? Why?

So many unanswered questions and every time I asked Him, God was silent. I searched the scripture – surely there was some meaning in all that had been done to me, and in all that I had done. For the longest time, I just kept coming up blank.   No answers. But I needed to understand.   So, I persisted, like the widow, who kept pestering the judge.

As a child, I was so innocent.   I didn't fully understand what was happening to me, when my innocence was being stolen. All I knew was the shame that enveloped me.   I kept asking, "Where were you God!?".   In my younger years, I would ask this question in anger, and I wondered, did it break His heart to see what was happening to me?   Did God really care or was I being tossed away – of no value to Him?   There were so many kids in the world - was I disposable?   These questions plagued me for most of my young life.   Now here I was, free in my spirit! The weight I had carried for so many years had been lifted.   But, yet - I still had no answers. What now?

While contemplating these questions and journaling, one evening, I heard God ask me, "Do you believe I love you?".   I paused and responded, "Sure, Lord!   Look how far you've brought me – surely you love me".   Again, He said, "Do you truly, believe that I love you?". As I sat there thinking about it, I realized that even though He had delivered me and forgave me, I still had a lingering doubt about whether He truly loved me. Isn't that nuts!?! After ALL He had brought me through – for heaven's sake, I'm free! How could I not believe that He loved me!?!   But I had to face it – I didn't – I didn't TRULY believe that He loved me. Crazy, isn't it?

I fell on my face and prayed so hard, my chest hurt.   I asked Him to help me to know, that not only did He love me, but to help me love Him in return, the way that He wants me to. His answer to me that night was to go to the source; His Word. I opened my Bible and flipped to the back, where there was a topical reference list.   I found the L's and looked for the word "Love".   There it was, with a huge list of references. I began my journey through the Bible, searching for God's love.

The search began in *Genesis 39:21*, Joseph was in prison for a crime he didn't commit. I knew the story – read it so many times in my childhood.   But the words seemed contradictory.   He's in prison, but *"The Lord was with Joseph and showed him mercy, and He gave him favor"*. It doesn't make sense, right? God had marked Joseph's life in childhood – blessed him with prophetic dreams - yet He allowed his brothers to sell him into slavery. But now, he was in prison because he tried to live righteous and ran from Potiphar's wife when she tried to seduce him! I found myself relating to Joseph's plight. A kid, anointed by God, unjustly treated, in a prison (mine was a mental prison), and sexual abuse was involved.

As I kept reading, I saw how God was with Him through every situation. He made Joseph a favorite with the prison warden. He put him in charge and caused everything he did to succeed. God was faithful to Joseph. So, what was different from his story compared to mine?

Then God's conviction fell on me - Joseph stayed faithful to God, no matter what he endured. I, however, did not. When life threw hard stuff at me, I made the choice to fall into pity and anger and every other, ugly emotion I could conjur. God was showing me, it was MY CHOICES that led me down the path I had taken. While Joseph chose righteousness, regardless of the situation he found himself in, I took the opposite path. I chose unrighteousness.

Next, he confirmed this understanding when we landed in *Exodus 20:6 I lavish my love – unfailing love – for a thousand*

generations on those who love me and obey my commands.
There was another key word, OBEY. Again, instead of choosing
obedience regardless of my situation, I chose rebellion.

Moving on, we landed in *Numbers 14:18 The LORD is slow
to anger, abounding in love and forgiving sin and rebellion. Yet
he does not leave the guilty unpunished.* Here again, He
confirmed His love, through His patience. But, along with that
love, comes discipline for our sins and rebellion against God. Yet,
He forgives, over and over and over and over. I noted in my
journal that night, "None who treat God with contempt will receive
His blessing. It was my anger towards God that caused me to
forfeit His blessings for so long." It was starting to click. His
Word was revealing the truth – the answers to the questions I had
been asking all along.

It all began with my choice – that first choice to not forgive
and to allow that root of anger and bitterness to take root. But I
was a kid, right? I didn't know better, right? Well, Joseph was a
kid too. Just as God was with Joseph, all those years, He was there
with me too. I detailed how many times, He tried to reach out to
me, but my stubborn anger and self-centeredness, both as a child, a
teenager, and as an adult, pushed Him away. Again, it was MY
choice, not God's. Even as I write this, I'm choking up, thinking
of how much He really, did love me, that even with ALL the filth
of my past - He still pursued me. He was waiting there in the
wings, until I came to the end of myself. That old saying,

"Sometimes you have to hit rock bottom, to look up". I hit it hard, and when I looked up, there was my God, waiting for me.

I continued, on my journey through the scripture, looking up every single verse that had the word "love" in it. In my journal, I wrote the main concept of the verse and how it applied to my life. The theme of God's unfailing love continued. He is always there, loving us, waiting for us to come to Him, reaching out to draw us to Him. But He also expects obedience and trust, and wholehearted love from us in return. Again, it always circled back to the choice I made. The choice to believe the lies of the enemy. The choice to be selfish, self-centered, egotistical… Think of every ugly verb possible, and it will describe who I had been.

I pressed on. ***Psalms 51:1***, from my notes: ***God's love is merciful – even though we rebel, God forgives and does not withhold His love. The sacrifice He desires is a broken spirit.*** Well, you got me there, Lord. You broke me.

Verse after verse confirmed His unfailing love for me.

Ps 89:14 Righteousness and justice are the foundation of your throne. Unfailing love and truth walk before you as attendants.

Ps 100:5 For the LORD is good. His unfailing love continues forever, and his faithfulness continues to each generation.

Ps 103:17 But the love of the LORD remains forever with those who fear him. His salvation extends to the children's children

Ps 106:1 Praise the LORD! Give thanks to the LORD, for he is good! His faithful love endures forever.

Ps 107:1 Give thanks to the LORD, for he is good! His faithful love endures forever.

Again, in my notes I commented: "God continually demonstrates His love for us; sometimes it hurts, but the suffering helps us to grow". There it was – suffering. We grow through suffering.

I don't like suffering – pretty sure, no one does. But God was showing me, it is necessary. He knew me, better than I knew myself. He knew the choices I would make, but He also knew, with my strong will, what it would take to break me – to get me to where He could use me. Now, someone who doesn't know God, will likely choke on that comment. There was a day, when I would have choked on it, as well. It's true, He allows suffering to come into our lives to break us, to increase us and to draw us to Him, so that we can be useful to the eternal kingdom. This world does not revolve around me! This world does not revolve around you! A person immersed in this world doesn't have an eternal mindset, so this whole concept will not make sense to them at all!   A Christian with rebellion in their heart, will likely not take that statement too kindly, either.   Regardless, it is truth!

Another truth He showed me that night, is that He too suffers, in our suffering.   He had already sent His son to pay for all my sins.   God Himself suffered watching His son being brutalized. For many years, I rejected Christ. Isaiah 63:9 tells us that His love and mercy redeemed us – paid the price for our sins. But every time we reject Jesus, it's like we're nailing Him to the cross again. You think that doesn't hurt God?   I'm convinced it does. God yearns for our love – He yearns for us to trust Him. Think about that – the Almighty yearns to be loved, just as we yearn to be loved.   In my spirit, I knew that God cried for me, each time I was being abused. But He has **forever vision** – He saw down through the years – He knew my stubbornness and pride and He knew exactly what it would take to bring me to the point of submission.

Those were some hard truths to swallow.   The reality is that God could have wiped me from the face of this earth at any point along the way, and He would have been justified in doing so.   I had made some really, wicked choices. But just as His Word told me, through my journey to understand His love, He is merciful and compassionate – slow to anger – filled with unfailing love – EAGER to turn back from destroying His people (Jonah 4:2). From Genesis to Revelations, over and over, He confirmed His love for me.

I had a decision to make. Do I choose to believe that God loves me? My answer was YES! I know, beyond a shadow of a doubt, that He loves me! And through this journey of love, I came to love Him with a sincere love and respect.

While God had brought me revelation and answers to some of my questions, He also convicted me that I needed to surrender all my "Why's?", now and forevermore, and to trust His heart for me. So, I did just that; I laid all my "Why's?" at the foot of the cross. I surrendered my need to have answers to all the questions. I may never understand, but that's ok. I no longer feel the need or desire to know why. What I know, is that He knows, and in that knowledge, I rest.

I choose daily to trust God above all else – regardless of the circumstances. He has been faithful to me – He IS faithful to me daily. He has provided for me and my children all these years. He has protected us all along the way. He pursued me and pulled me away from death many times. He broke me. He healed me. He loves me.

21 CONTENTMENT

I am thankful for the wounds that pushed me back towards God. The verse in *1 Timothy 6:6*, where the Apostle Paul talks about contentment is for real – it is possible. The world will tell us otherwise, but God has proven it out in my life. Though I'm still single, I'm not alone. Though I was severely damaged as a child, I am healed. Though I committed horrendous atrocities against God and my own flesh and blood, I am forgiven. Though I was unlovable, I am loved. Though I was in chains, I am free!

I read something online, by the author, Lysa TerKeurst, where she stated, "Scars are not imperfections. They are fascinating survival stories waiting to be told". She was talking about her scars from cancer, but this statement so applies to internal, emotional and spiritual scars as well. Think about it, scars are sealed up, healed. They're just a sign that a wound had existed. My scars had once been open, festering, wounds. But now, they're just scars. They're still there but sealed up and no longer oozing the putrid, vile, ugliness that had once been so prevalent in my life. My scars no longer have power over my life or my future. I could feel God was moving me into an entirely new phase of life. He had become the power over my life and future.

He was using me, more and more, to counsel others who were broken – they were my training grounds. One such broken woman, crossed my path that same year. She had married a

Muslim man and was in the middle of a divorce. She fell into a severe depression and, with the absence of the true God in her life, in her desperation, she attempted suicide. She ended up losing custody of both of her children. God allowed me the opportunity to minister to her – to teach her about the power of forgiveness. Praise God, she found the healing she needed. First, by accepting Christ as her Savior, and then by humbling herself and seeking the spiritual and psychological counseling she desperately needed.

God continued to work on me as well. I felt in my spirit that God had big plans in the work – it was like a tingling in my senses that I couldn't explain. Next up – my ex-husband. Again? Seriously! Yes, this time God wanted me to let him (the ex) know that he was released. Say what!?! I'm pretty, sure that wasn't the "big plan" I was hoping for, but there it was.

It was around New Year's, 2011, when my niece contacted me, saying Ed had reached out to her. He wanted to contact me. The courts had caught up to him and apparently, put the fear of God in him. He had recently remarried and was trying to straighten out his life. He had not paid for any of the insurance or child support. The courts were telling him he had to cover at least one child with insurance. So, he was trying to contact me to discuss that. My niece provided him an email address that he could use to contact me. And he did – he explained what the court had said. I advised him, it was already taken care of – I had made sure the kids were covered all those years.

I was wondering if through the exchanges, he would ever apologize for abandoning his kids and me. He did not. However, after the "business" was concluded, God convicted me that I had one more email to send. This time, I had to let him know, I had released him from what he had done to me and the kids – regardless of the fact, that he had not apologized or sought to make anything right with me or them. I had already chosen to forgive the man – this just didn't make sense!

It was painful. I prayed and asked the Holy Spirit to give me the words, because everything I wrote (in my humanness), I had to keep deleting. I'm pretty, sure what I originally wrote was NOT what the Lord had in mind. Even though I had already forgiven him, my flesh still wanted to give him a piece of my mind! But God is faithful and after much prayer, He gave me the right words to say. In obedience, I composed the email and apologized to him for all the times I had failed him during the marriage. I humbled myself and asked Ed to forgive me. I didn't accuse or place blame, like my flesh at first wanted to. Instead, I conceded my own failures. When I clicked SEND on that email, the relief was immediate. The weight of the world was lifted off my shoulders. I seriously felt like I was walking on air for days afterwards! I had a new joy and inner peace that I'm not sure I can ever convey by words.

Contentment had become my new buzzword. What's amazing is that it only took me getting rid of more of the junk that

I kept trying to carry around. What it took, was learning to "die to self". The old self was dead, but I found myself more alive and more aware of God and true life, than I could have ever dreamed before.

I realized that I may never hear, "I'm sorry" from Ed or any man for that matter – although Ford's apology on behalf of all men, was an excellent stand-in. But, in order to experience the fullness of God, I had to let it ALL go. I knew then that if God impressed on me to surrender hurt feelings and expectations of someone else, making it right, then that's exactly what I had to do, and immediately! He wants no hesitation in obedience! Experiencing that level of freedom after forgiving Ed, reinforced that in my mind. I know now that forgiveness, obedience, and contentment, go hand in hand. That is surrender.

1 Timothy 6:6-11 But godliness with contentment is great gain.

22 NEW ADVENTURES!

As I mentioned earlier, I sensed a stirring in the heavenlies – I knew God was getting ready to make a big move in my life. I've got to back up and lay the ground work for what I knew He was getting ready to do. When I was eighteen years old, I had my first job, and bought a new car. My older brother, Sam, had asked to borrow it, to drive to Jacksonville, North Carolina, to pick up his sister-in-law. At this point, I had only been to Kentucky and Ohio, and was desperate to see more of the world. So, I agreed, he could use it, if I got to ride along. It was a life changing trip, in that, I completely fell in love with the state of North Carolina. I said to my brother and his wife, Robin, that I was going to move to that state. Of course, no one took me seriously. But over the years, when I wasn't busy pushing God out of my life, I was busy asking Him to help me achieve the dream of moving to NC, some day. Thirty years later, that prayer was answered.

In March of 2011, (a year after I gained my freedom!) at another Christian gathering I attended with Vareena, another woman approached me and said she had a prophetic Word from God for me. I had never experienced that before, but I thought ok, let's hear it. She told me, that the Holy Spirit said I would be making a transition – a geographical move!

Philippians 2:13 For it is God who works in you to will and to act according to his good purpose.

Needless to say, I was thrilled!   Instantly, I said "North Carolina, here I come!".   To the woman I said, "He meant North Carolina – right?!".   But no, He only said "geographical".   However, I was bent on the Carolinas, so that's what I received.   Vareena rejoiced with me – I had shared with her many times, my desire to move south.   I knew in my spirit, that God would somehow, some way, open doors for me to make this move.   I can't explain the draw that I had felt towards the state of North Carolina, but I now believe, that it was God that planted that seed long ago and drew me here.   I believed then and still do, that it was His will.

In August of 2011, I had put my house in Ohio, up for sale.   I got regular viewings, but no offers.   I left it on the market for a year.   In August of 2012, I unlisted it.   I had been searching for a job in North Carolina for months but had no luck.   Every door got slammed on me as soon as they figured out, I was in Ohio.   The economy was still in a slump and no one wanted to pay for relocation.   Aaron had graduated high school in 2010, and Autumn graduated that June 2012.   I felt the timing was good for us to make the move.   All three of us loved the state.   We vacationed there every year and talked of moving to NC often.

I committed it to prayer and surrendered it to God.   Afterall, I truly believed God had told me that it was going to happen.   So, it was a matter of faith – I had to choose to believe that God would guide me.   He had given me the desire.   He had given me confirmation, both in my spirit and by way of the woman who approached me. But I also knew that God works in His own time, and He can't be rushed. While I knew it was going to happen, I just didn't know when. So, I waited.

God's timing is perfect. When we find ourselves in the middle of hard times, it's often hard to see Him working. It's only when looking back that we see how God so finely, knit everything together. On July 3, 2012, around 10:30pm, we received some sad news. My brother, Billy Ray, had just passed away. He lived two blocks from me. The kids and I piled into the car and raced over to his house. The medics had just left after pronouncing him dead. He had fallen asleep in his recliner, and it appeared, he had peacefully passed in his sleep. Billy had a plethora of health issues, but we're pretty sure it was his heart that just gave out. We had been told 35 years earlier, that he wouldn't last out the year, but here it was 35 years later, when God took him. We were blessed to have him for as long as we did.

He lay there on the floor, where they had moved him. The look on his face was of peace, not pain. My brother, JR and his wife, Irene, who lived with him, were there, along with one of our nieces. Our sister, Paulette and her son arrived shortly afterwards. Later, another sister, Darlene, came. We sat there with his body until the funeral home arrived to pick him up, at 1:30am. It was a painful three hours. A few days later, we buried him in Kentucky. I'm thankful to report that Billy had given his heart to Jesus when I was a teenager. So, I know, I'll see him again, one day. There is a reason, I included the information about my brother's passing, which will become evident, later in this story, as everything in God's timing is perfect, though very sad in that we lost our beloved brother.

It was around Christmas-time that year, I remember clearly, God speaking to me. He said, "Get your house in order". I knew exactly what He meant. There were a couple of minor fixes I had to do on my house. I knew He was telling me, it's time to re-list it – the move is on! So, I spent the next couple of weeks taking care of the fixes and staging the house for showings.

On January 18, 2013, I contracted with a new realtor. On January 20th, she took pictures of my home. On January 21st, she listed my home on MLS. We ended up with showings every day that week. On January 29th, eight days after listing it on MLS, I accepted an offer on the home and we had a signed contract! I don't know about you, but that still gives me Holy Ghost chills! Everything was in God's timing!

However, there was a looming issue - I didn't have a job in North Carolina! Oops! But God had told me to get ready, so I had to trust that He had a plan! Everything in my spirit and all the cues around me were pointing to God's will in this move. The only thing I had not consulted at this point, was His Word. I knew I needed to get the confirmation from the Bible, that I was on the right path. I prayed and asked Him to confirm that this indeed, was His plan. In my quiet time that morning, I was studying in Genesis and there it was – the confirmation I had asked him to provide. ***Genesis 12:1 The LORD had said to Abram, 'Go from your country, your people and your father's household to the land I will show you'.***. Ask and ye shall receive. After that, I had no doubt in my spirit that this truly was God's plan for me. I pressed forward, in faith!

The following Friday night, my daughter and I climbed in my car, and we headed to Asheville, North Carolina, to look around and determine where we wanted to move. We spent the weekend looking at homes and the area. While I had peace that North Carolina was the state, I didn't have peace that Asheville or its surrounding areas was the place where He intended to plant us. We went back home and planned our next visit – this time to Charlotte, North Carolina. We had been to Charlotte before and were already in love with it.

The following weekend, we made the trek back down to Charlotte. I had contacted a realtor and she had six houses lined up for us to view. We arrived on Friday and all but one of the houses had been contracted during the week. The only one remaining was not what I was looking for. I felt God moving me to find a place to rent. It made sense. It would allow us to get acclimated to the area and figure out where we really, wanted to live. I could take my time finding the right house to buy.

We set out to find a rental – which ended up not being that easy to do. Several homes we looked at didn't allow big dogs and well, we had Lacy Sunshine, a 90-pound, black Retriever. She had been part of our family for 13 years and there was no way we were going to part with her. We continued our search, all weekend long. By Sunday, evening, we hadn't found anything that worked for us. Three adults, a dog and a cat. It shouldn't be that hard. But every time we thought we were close, either someone just beat us to it, or it was the "big dog" or the "cat" issue. I took off an extra day, so we could extend our stay thru Monday and drive back to Ohio on Monday night. As of Monday, at noon, still no luck. I was feeling a bit desperate. I had that sense of urgency, so I knew this was God moving me to find a place. I kept telling myself, "Have faith – God's got this!".

We had been all over the Charlotte area. As we drove up 77 north, I just started to pray out loud in the car. My prayer was that I knew in my spirit, this was His will – I had prayed and had peace, I got confirmation from a stranger, who prophesied to me, I got godly counsel from trusted friends and they had peace, and God led me to scripture that confirmed this was His doing. So, now, I need Him to direct my path to the place where we would live – and that they would allow our big dog and cat! My daughter, who's "not into God", just looked at me kind of odd, but I HAD to cry out to Abba. Honestly, I should have started with that prayer – pretty sure, I could have saved myself a lot of stress and mileage on my car if I had. But everything happens for a reason!

I finished my prayer, and one mile ahead, there was an exit for Huntersville. I felt the spirit tell me to take that exit. Ok – done – took the exit. Now what? Again, I heard Him clear as day, "Turn left". Ok –done. Now what? "Drive." So, I drove West on Route 73 and off to the right was an apartment complex – very nice one too. As I got closer to it, I again heard the spirit, "Turn right into the apartments". So, I did, and there right in front of me was a sign saying "Vacancies – Big Dogs Welcome"!!! Whoo-hoo! Autumn and I were both doing the happy dance! Even though I had no idea if they had the size apartment we needed or allowed cats, I knew God had it all worked out.

I went into the office, told the lady we were looking for a 3-bedroom rental, starting on March 1st and we needed a lease for 6 months (that was the number God gave me when I prayed), we have a big dog and a cat, and three humans. She smiled big and said, "You're in luck! We have only one 3-bedroom unit that JUST became available, and absolutely, you can have a 6-month lease!". All pets AND humans - are welcome!". Now keep in mind, no one else was willing to give us a 6-month lease, and no other place we had visited had a 3-bedroom available, and there was either the dog or the cat issue. Now, tell me that wasn't God and I will tell you, it undoubtedly was Him!!! We viewed the unit, which had the same square footage as the house I was selling in Ohio. So, it was perfect. I had never lived in a rental or an apartment for that matter, so this was a new experience and I like trying new things. I signed the lease, paid the deposits, and Autumn and I drove home to Ohio that evening, content that the plan was fully in motion! However, there's still that pesky issue about the job - I didn't have one in North Carolina!

I went to work on Tuesday with an idea, which I believe God had planted in my head as I drove home the prior night. I worked from home quite often with my current job. They had allowed me to alter my hours so that I could home-school both of my kids and I had done that for seven years. It worked perfectly. Why would Evenflo not allow me to work from home in North Carolina – permanently!?! So, I approached one of the other managers in the department. We both reported to the same Director, but even though I had known him longer, she knew him better. I told her about the house sale, the apartment rental, the lack of a job in NC, and the idea of me working from home and keeping my current job. She thought it was a great idea and she counseled me on how to approach our boss.

I prayed and had peace in my spirit that this was God's plan. So, I booked a meeting with my boss the following week. The day came for us to meet. I sat down across from him and shared that I had sold my house. He congratulated me and asked where I was moving to (fully assuming it was in the surrounding area). I blurted out, "North Carolina". He looked stunned. Now, I know Evenflo could have survived without me. But at that point, I had been there for 17 years and my boss, heavily depended on me and my knowledge of the systems and processes. My leaving would have been bumpy for them - for a while. I went on to tell him I had already rented an apartment and would be moving there in March. He assumed I had another job already and was quite confused when I told him I didn't, but that I had an idea that I wanted to run past him. We discussed my working from home in North Carolina, and coming back to Ohio, for a week, every few weeks. He thought that was a great idea and said he would take it up the ladder to get approvals.

Take it up the ladder, he did. Both the CFO and the CEO signed off on it. The only caveat was that I had to spend at least one week per month in the Ohio office. Easy enough – deal was done – we put the arrangement in writing, and all was well. God is good, is He not!?! Later, my boss, asked me what I would have done if they had not agreed. I simply told him, I'd be in Ohio Monday through Friday, until I found another job in Charlotte. I knew in my gut that with a NC address, I'd have no problem getting another job there. But, after everything transpired, I know it was God's will for me to continue with Evenflo. And it has worked out very well for almost six years, as of this writing.

Everything didn't go off without a hitch with the move – there were a few bumps in the road along the process. For instance, a certain, racoon, in the motherly way, decided my attic was her new birthing unit. The damage she created breaking into my house, cost me a pretty penny – not to mention the cost of having her, and her little ones, evicted. Then, the new buyers, were going through FHA for financing, so there were several battles with the FHA trying to force me to make further "improvements" to the home, at my cost. It was a 100-year old house. I had already replaced all exterior doors and 90% of the windows in the house. I refused to replace any more but contracted with a company to fix one of the larger windows – again, a significant cost. That calmed the beast FHA, at least briefly. Next, the FHA weren't happy with the agreed upon price of the home. So, to continue with the process, I had to drop my price by a few thousand, to match the appraised amount. So, this meant, less money for the move. My savings had been depleted with the unexpected fixes and, now the price drop. But I was at peace. I knew God had a plan.

The financial concerns for the move were laid to rest when as a surprise to me and my siblings, our brother, Billy, had left us each a sizable, inheritance. It was an unexpected gift. The amount I received fully covered the cost of our move to North Carolina. It's hard to fathom that God had worked out the details, so intricately. He knew long before Billy passed, when his time would be. He knew long before I began the transition to North Carolina, exactly when it would be and all the things that would happen that consumed the funds I had put aside and planned for the move. Yet everything was orchestrated, in His perfect timing. All the finances were covered. Thank you, God and thank you for the gift, Billy. I knew that if I kept my focus on God and His will, every step of the way, He would direct my path.

Proverbs 3:4-6 Then you will find favor and high regard in the sight of God and man. Trust in the LORD with all your heart, and lean not on your own understanding; in all your ways acknowledge Him, and He will make your paths straight.

I felt God's tangible presence through the whole process. I got to witness of His goodness to many people along the way. The realtor was amazed every time she called with an issue and my response, would be, "OK, we'll work it out – God is directing this move, and He'll give me the solution". Every time, He did just that.

23 WRITE THE BOOK!

I started working on this book during this past summer and as I'm wrapping this up, it's now, early December 2018. Which means it was 50-years ago this month that my spiritual journey began. It's been almost six years since we moved to the Charlotte area of North Carolina. In that time, God guided me in locating a piece of land and in building a new home, which we moved into five years ago this month. When we moved here, I knew no one. But God in his love and mercy, has led many wonderful friends into my life. He led me into ministry again here in North Carolina. I've led a Life Group for the past three years and He's used me to mentor, encourage and love these wonderful friends He brought into my life.

I know He was drawing me here for a purpose and part of that purpose was to lead me – for this season - into fellowship with a group of people, who are intent on living their faith out loud. No secrets – freely confessing their hearts to each other with no judgement - which is what I have craved for so long. It was through the Women's ministries at Pursuit Church, in Denver, NC, under the leadership and example, of Terri Broome, that I saw people coming clean about their past, with no fear of judgement or condemnation. It was their fearlessness – first modeled by Terri - that convicted me that it was time for me to face up to my past.

Matthew 10:26-28 Nothing hidden not revealed,

no secret not made known

1 Corinthians 4:5 Who will bring to light the hidden things of

darkness and reveal the counsel of the heart.

Ps 19:12-14 But who can discern their own errors? Forgive my

hidden faults.   Keep your servant also from willful sins; may

they not rule over me. Then I will be blameless, innocent of great

transgression.   May these words of my mouth and this meditation

of my heart be pleasing in your sight, LORD,

my Rock and my Redeemer.

For the past 20 years, I knew in my heart, it was only a matter of time, until God would require me to expose the sins of my past, painful as that may be.   I truly believe that had I not allowed Him to do the work in me, I would not be here to share my story today. I was on the quick road to death and He delivered me.   In Joel 2:25-26 God promises, He will restore the years that the locust has eaten.   He has restored so much in my life.   For Him to continue to do that, I must trust Him to do whatever He needs to do in me and through me.   That starts with obedience.   He told me to write this, so I obeyed.

If we suffer, and learn from our suffering, and then keep the miracles of what we learned to ourselves – sure, we will profit spiritually from the growth - but God's intention is that what we learn through our suffering be shared with others, who need Him as desperately as I did. I had the advantage of being raised by godly parents, who taught me God's Word. God used those truths that were embedded in my brain to call to me. There are many folks today, who've never heard the Word of God - but they might pick up a book by someone, obscure and unknown, like me, out of curiosity. So, if something in my story can reach into the heart of another person that is on the path I was on, then what I went through would not be in vain. For this reason, it's vital that I come clean and share all the dirty details of how God pulled me from the pit of despair and put me on the path of a Holy Spirit-filled life!

So, how did I come to write my story, at this time? Well, around fifteen years ago, I had put together a Bible study, titled "God in the Workplace", where I shared many truths that God had revealed to me about how we Christians are to walk out our faith in the workplace. The folks I was leading at that time, really enjoyed it. I felt the Holy Spirit tell me to put it in writing – in a book. But I promptly ignored that nudge and didn't obey Him.

This past summer, I found myself struggling with some of the same issues that God had taught me those many years before. I was frustrated – couldn't find peace in my job and couldn't put my finger on the source of the problem. Finally, while praying one day, I said to God, "Lord, what's the deal!?! I've been down this road before and I'm doing my best to put into practice all the principals you taught me! Why have I lost my contentment?".

As always, God is faithful to answer. The first thing that popped into my head was "the book". Ugh – the book! I had been disobedient, and God had brought me back, full circle. Not only that, but a key verse that continually popped out at me was **Psalm 119:60 I hasten and do not delay to keep your commandments**. Clearly, the hastening part, I failed – epically! My prayer became, **Psalm 143:10 Teach me to do your will, for you are my God! Let your good Spirit lead me on level ground!** I repented, asked for forgiveness, and began looking for my notebooks.

In the move from Ohio, I seemed to have lost a tub of my study notes. So, I told God He'd just have to give me a fresh word on what He wanted included. I began to make my outline for recreating the study and at first, it was going very smoothly. It seemed like the best "downloads" from God came, as my head hit the pillow each night. I had to keep a notepad and pen, and eventually my laptop by my bedside, so I wouldn't lose the information that was flooding my brain. But after a couple weeks, it stopped – the downloads from God – it all dried up.

I prayed and asked God to help me – this was His idea anyways, right!?! Well, He did help, but instead of leading me to continue with the "Workplace" book, He began filling my head with memories of my spiritual journey – this story, you've just read. I knew in my spirit, that He wanted me to start with putting my story into print.

So, I tabled the "Workplace" book temporarily, and began the journey of exposing my heart and soul. Coming clean about my past has been painfully (emphasis added), liberating, to say the least. I have shed many tears as I compiled these pages. But the tears are from joy instead of heartbreak. My hope is that through my journey from pain, rebellion, and utter depravity, to healing, forgiveness, restoration, hope, mercy and love; that others who have found themselves on the same path, may be encouraged, to find their way out of the black abyss.

24 THE POTTER

I was reading in Jeremiah recently and ran across the story of the Potter's House.   Through this story, I felt the conviction, of how my flesh is my constant reminder of how much I need to stay connected to God and to walk in complete obedience to Him.

Jeremiah 18:1-4 This is the word that came to Jeremiah from the LORD: 2 "Go down to the potter's house, and there I will give you my message." 3 So I went down to the potter's house, and I saw him working at the wheel. 4 But the pot he was shaping from the clay was marred in his hands; so, the potter formed it into another pot, shaping it as seemed best to him.

Early in my life, God had His original plan for me – He began to shape me and form in me a desire to serve Him - to fulfill the plan He had for me.   But the pot he was shaping (me) – became marred – not because of the Potter (God), but because of the pot's (my) resistance to His hands.   So, the Potter, shaped it into something else – something that seemed best to Him – maybe not the original plan – but what is now, best for both Him and me, and for His kingdom.   I am clay in His hands. My resistance to His original plan, altered the course of my life.   By my continual surrender to God's will, He continues to form me into a vessel that He can now use for His kingdom. My love and obedience to God, guarantees that He will only continue to build my life up and will protect me from the disaster that inevitably, was heading my way.

Earlier I made this statement and feel I need to reiterate it again.   Please hear my heart in this!   I **choose daily** to **trust God** above all else and to **remain** in Him and to be **faithful** to Him – **regardless of the circumstances**.   God has been faithful to me – God **IS** faithful to me.   He has provided for me and my children all these years.   He has protected us all along the way.   He pursued me and pulled me away from death many times**.   He broke me! He healed me!   He loves me!**

Please friend, allow God to do the same work in your heart.   If you don't feel pain or sorrow for the sin in your life, there's something desperately, wrong.   You have not gone as far as God wants to take you.   Please go to Him - ask Him to show you, to open your hard, heart and to lead you down the path of deliverance and healing, as ONLY GOD can do.   And then remain in Him - rest in Him.

Isaiah 61:1-3 The Spirit of the Sovereign LORD is upon me, for the LORD has anointed me to bring good news to the poor.   He has sent me to comfort the brokenhearted and to proclaim that captives will be <u>released</u> and prisoners will be <u>freed</u>.

2 He has sent me to tell those who mourn that the time of the LORD's favor has come, and with it, the day of God's anger against their enemies.

3 To all who mourn in Israel, he will give a crown of beauty for ashes, a joyous blessing instead of mourning, festive praise instead of despair.   In their righteousness, they will be like great oaks that the LORD has planted for his own glory.

25 THERE'S SOMETHING IN A NAME

Just one more, quirky little story I want to share. I've always been fascinated with the origins of names. My dad used to say they were important to God – they describe the character of the man.

When I was a kid, my family and friends called me by my middle name, Denise (or nick-name, Neicie). So, I looked up the origin of that name. The name Denise, comes from the Latin Dionysus, referring to the Greek **god of wine** – it implies drunkenness, revelry, rebellion and a false god. Ha! That was truly me!

However, when I was in college, my professors refused to call anyone by their middle name – only by their first. I became known to everyone as Allison. After I got out of college, I continued to introduce myself and go by the name, Allison. So, I looked it up and it too, had significant meaning to me. Alison/Allison has two etymologies. Alison and all its variations are from Alicen, a feminine French diminutive of Alice and from the Greek "Alethea" meaning – get this! - "**Truth**"!

So, there you have it folks! Just as God changed the name of Abram to Abraham, and Jacob to Israel, He changed mine too! In my transformation from the whoring, rebellious, murderous, hard-hearted, vixon, He changed me, Allison, into a God-fearing woman of TRUTH! I can live with that! Amen!

Zechariah 4:6 'Not by might nor by power, but by my Spirit,'

says the LORD Almighty.

May God's peace and grace be with you…

REFERENCES

Asian Peels, *Peeling Dragon Skin, Part 3 from Voyage of Dawntreader,* (2009, May 6) retrieved November, 2018, from https://peelingdragonskin.wordpress.com/tag/cs-lewis-quotes/

Bilger, M, *Abortion Activists Threaten to Rape, Kill Christian Woman Over Her Pro-Life Tweet* (2018, Sept 12) retrieved October, 2018 from https://www.lifenews.com/2018/09/12/abortion-activists-threaten-to-rape-kill-christian-woman-over-her-pro-life-tweet/

Buckingham, J. (1976) *Risky Living: Keys to Inner Healing* Plainfield, Logos International

Frangipane, F. (1989) *The Three Battlegrounds*, Cedar Rapids, Arrow Publications

Savard, L. (1992) *Shattering Your Strongholds*, North Brunswick, Bridge-Logos Publishers

ABOUT THE AUTHOR

The author, Allison Denise Pelphrey, resides in the Huntersville, NC area with her son, Aaron, and daughter, Autumn. Her passions include Christian ministry, hiking, camping and exploring the Blue Ridge Mountains. Allison is an avid reader and loves all animals, botanicals and gardening.

You can follow Allison on her blog: allisondpelphrey.com

Made in the USA
Columbia, SC
20 September 2019